GROWING DIVERSITY

Growing Diversity

Genetic resources and local food security

Edited by
DAVID COOPER, RENÉE VELLVÉ and HENK HOBBELINK

(*GRAIN*) *Genetic Resources Action International*
in co-operation with
Centro Internazionale Crocevia

INTERMEDIATE TECHNOLOGY PUBLICATIONS 1992

Intermediate Technology Publications
103/105 Southampton Row, London WC1B 4HH, UK

© IT Publications 1992

ISBN 1 85339 123 9 (Hardback)
ISBN 1 85339 119 0 (Paperback)

Typeset by Inforum Typesetting, Portsmouth
Printed in Great Britain by SRP, Exeter

Contents

Acknowledgements/About this book

The decision to produce a book reflecting grassroots experiences in genetic resources conservation and improvement was made jointly by several workers from NGOs active in the field in November 1989. A survey of some 50 development agencies, both official and from the voluntary sector, had shown that, while they considered genetic resources to be a very important aspect of development work, they lacked the concrete and practical information on how to incoporate genetic resources activities into the projects they support. This book is meant to be a first step towards filling the information gap. We hope that it will stimulate greater discussion with the aim of strengthening local conservation activities in the South.

Most of the contributors to the book are directly involved in grassroots activities with urgent and daily responsibilities to the communities with which they work. Despite their busy lives they have managed to produce these accounts of their experiences. Our first thanks therefore go to the authors for making this book possible. We are also indebted to all those involved in the global network whose cumulative activities, views and comments have provided the intellectual and philosophical background to this publication. Most have contributed in some way to this book and many of their ideas may be reflected here. We would like to thank the staff of Intermediate Technology Development Group (ITDG) and IT Publications for their helpful co-operation in the preparation of this book.

This project was initiated and co-ordinated by Genetic Resources Action International (GRAIN) in co-operation with Centro Internazionale Crocevia. GRAIN is supported financially by a range of aid agencies and governmental sources. We wish to thank all those who have supported our work during the last three years: Catholic Fund for Overseas Development (UK); CS Fund (USA); Danchurchaid (Denmark); Dutch Ministry of Development Co-operation; Misereor (Germany); Norwegian Ministry of Environment; Novib (Netherlands); Swedish International Development Authority; Swissaid (Switzerland); Trocaire (Ireland).

This book is meant to put an untold story on paper, and spread the impetus of further creativity, strength, co-operation and action. No contributor tries to give a blueprint on how things should work or what is the best model to promote conservation and breeding at the grassroots level. Rather, each talks about her or his work and the world they are up against, points out the constraints and raises an infinite number of questions and possibilities. In editing these papers, GRAIN has tried to leave intact each author's style of expression while focusing on the clarity of the message. We hope we have succeeded in this. It goes without saying, however, that the views expressed are solely those of the individual authors.

GRAIN
December 1991

1 Why farmer-based conservation and improvement of plant genetic resources?

Genetic Resources Action International (GRAIN)

Farmers have managed genetic resources for as long as they have cultivated crops. Over the past few decades, however, this management has been progressively shifted from their control. Now, alongside calls for sustainable agriculture, more and more people are recognizing the role of local communities and especially of small-scale farmers in development. In this introductory chapter, David Cooper, Henk Hobbelink and Renée Vellvé,* of GRAIN, describe the importance of genetic diversity and outline the role farming communities play in its conservation. They describe how the Green Revolution has accelerated genetic erosion, and undermined farmers' efforts to conserve and improve their traditional varieties. They also point to new openings at the international level which provide for possible changes in the current approach to genetic resources management and conclude with ideas on how to turn the trend.

Why diversity?

For many farming communities, diversity, be it social, cultural, economic or genetic, means security. Genetic diversity provides security for the farmer against pests, disease and unexpected climatic conditions. It also helps small-scale farmers to maximize production in the highly variable

---

* David Cooper is an agricultural scientist working with GRAIN on biodiversity policy. He has been working with non-governmental organizations (NGOs) on public information and campaigning work for many years and is a member of Council of the World Development Movement. Henk Hobbelink, an agronomist, is the founder and co-ordinator of GRAIN. He is one of the leading NGO activists campaigning on genetic resources and biotechnology and is the author of *Biotechnology and the Future of World Agriculture*. Renée Vellvé is currently the Programme Officer of GRAIN. Previously she worked with European NGOs on the conservation of genetic resources and the impact of the new biotechnologies.

environments in which they tend to cultivate their crops. Higher yields are obtained from employing a mixture of crops and crop varieties, each one specifically adapted to the micro-environment in which it grows, rather than by using one or few 'modern' varieties. Such uniform varieties will only reach their potential if the environment is also uniform. That means high quality land, where the fertility and water status have been evened out with the use of fertilizers and irrigation, all generally unavailable to the small-scale farmer.

Besides often giving higher yields than crop uniformity for farmers in marginal areas, genetic diversity provides farming communities with a range of products with multiple uses. Some varieties of a particular crop may be good for immediate consumption, others for long-term storage, for example. This genetic wealth is, in addition, an important reservoir of diversity for agriculture worldwide, providing important and valuable characteristics for pest and disease resistance, nutritional quality and other factors, to meet both predictable and unforeseen ecological and economic circumstances.

Based on thousands of years of experience and a deep knowledge of their needs and their agricultural production systems, communities have developed multiple strategies for their farming systems, almost all of which maintain genetic diversity. Traditionally, small-scale farmers not only use a wide range of crop species in their complex agricultural systems of intercropping and agroforestry, but they use several varieties of each crop. For cereals like sorghum, rice, wheat and barley, which are self-pollinated, and for vegetatively propagating crops like potatoes and bananas, the number of varieties used may be very high. Further to this, farmers' traditional varieties tend to have a greater inherent, intra-varietal diversity than modern ones, especially for species such as maize and millet.

Several of the contributions in this book set out the diversity of varieties traditionally employed by farmers. Camila Montecinos and Miguel Altieri (Chapter 10) give examples of the occurrence and utilization of inter- and intra-varietal diversity in traditional Latin American farming systems and show how farmers produce new varieties by crossing with wild and weedy relatives. In the Chiloe islands off South America, for example, 146 varieties of potato are found. This enormous genetic diversity of crop plants has been created by such innovation and experimentation of farmers. Other examples are given by Rene Salazar (Chapter 2) and Pat Mooney (Chapter 12).

While the public imagination in industrialized countries is dominated by concern for the biological diversity of the tropical rainforest ecosystems, that in the farmers' field is at least as significant in human terms since it underpins our basic food security. Nowhere does the diversity within traditional cropping systems assume more significance than in the centres of origin and diversity of the world's major food crops. Most of these centres are located in what are now developing countries, including some of the poorest in the world (Figure 1). The rich North, by contrast, is genetically very poor. Most of the important food crops cultivated in the industrialized countries have origins in the Third World, which continues to subsidize Northern agriculture through the supply of genes for pest and disease resistance and other characteristics, estimated to be worth several billions of dollars a year according to the Organization for Economic Cooperation and Development (OECD). And most of the genetic diversity of the Third World is maintained and developed by small-scale farmers.

The Green Revolution: destroying diversity

One reason that attention is now being focused on the work of farmer-based systems of genetic resource conservation and use is that the problems and shortcomings of the formal approach are being recognized. Thirty years ago, the US-based Rockefeller and Ford foundations launched what was to become known as the Green Revolution, based on the paradigm that science could feed the hungry. The initial effects of the technological improvements gave spectacular increases in yield of staple cereals like maize and rice, and, building on this success, a network of International Agricultural Research Centres (IARCs) was created. These early advances in output were achieved by two quickly exploited techniques: reducing plant height, so more energy is devoted to grain production, and employing chemical fertilizers and irrigation. But by concentrating on this approach, which requires optimum production conditions, the IARCs are now unlikely to be able to serve the myriad complexities of marginal areas and the extreme heterogeneity which characterize

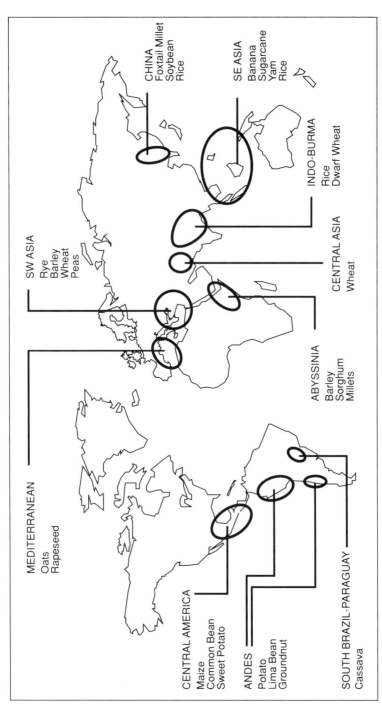

Figure 1. *Map of the Centres of Genetic Diversity based on those identified by V. I. Vavilov showing the principal origins and centres of diversity of twenty major crops. These account for about 90 per cent of the world's food supply (calorific intake).*

MEDITERRANEAN
Oats
Rapeseed

SW ASIA
Rye
Barley
Wheat
Peas

CHINA
Foxtail Millet
Soybean
Rice

SE ASIA
Banana
Sugarcane
Yam
Rice

INDO-BURMA
Rice
Dwarf Wheat

CENTRAL ASIA
Wheat

ABYSSINIA
Barley
Sorghum
Millets

CENTRAL AMERICA
Maize
Common Bean
Sweet Potato

ANDES
Potato
Lima Bean
Groundnut

SOUTH BRAZIL-PARAGUAY
Cassava

4

their soil structures, micro-climates and other aspects of their agro-ecological systems.

Besides these limitations, the high-tech package of the Green Revolution approach has led to other well-known problems; many examples appear in this book. The genetic uniformity of the miracle seeds and the chemical-intensive technology involved was giving rise to major outbreaks of pests and diseases leading to disastrous crop failures (see Chapters 2 and 3, for example). Equally bad, as the new seeds replaced the old traditional varieties and their wild relatives, the plant breeding's future raw material was being lost. Although the Green Revolution usually refers to the initial wave of scientific intervention into Third World agriculture, the same sort of policies have been continued more or less unaltered since.

The real tragedy of the Green Revolution is that it undermined, and in many cases destroyed, farmers' practices based on diversity. In its push for uniformity it not only destroyed much of the diversity of genetic resources in the farmers' fields, but it also disrupted the sophisticated biological chains that form the basis of any sustainable agriculture (see Chapter 5). In all this, it affected profoundly the capacity of millions of farmers to survive with the limited means at their disposal. By moving technology from village to laboratory and germplasm from field to genebank, the Green Revolution has tended to reduce farmers' control over their own production systems.

Genebanks: freezing diversity

The answer to the problem of genetic erosion coming from the 'formal' system of research institutes and professional breeders has been to establish genebanks to store samples of displaced or threatened varieties. Genebanks are effectively giant refrigerators where samples of seeds or other propagative materials of plants are kept under controlled conditions of temperature and humidity. Periodically, part of the sample is bred out and new seed produced, to rejuvenate and replace the sample. The concept is simple but as the primary tool for conservation it is seriously flawed. The emphasis is really not one of conservation in the true sense, but rather of preservation of seed samples maintained separately from agricultural production. Therefore the evolutionary processes which otherwise ensure sustained adaptation to changing environmental and social conditions are frozen out. Another major problem is that we know very little about the varieties stored in genebanks and even less about their potential uses. Divorced from their agro-ecological origins, rarely will we have information about the complex interactions of the variety in question with other aspects of the farming system. The problem of lack of knowledge about the material stored in genebanks is so serious that plant breeders hardly ever call on genebanks for new materials. The genebank approach is failing even the formal system itself. Conservation is effectively cut off not only from use in production, but also from improvement through breeding.

Added to these technical drawbacks of conservation through genebanks has been a number of political difficulties. From the mid-1970s the leadership of and control over germplasm collection and the establishment of a global genebank system was entrusted to the International Board for Plant Genetic Resources (IBPGR), created a few years earlier amid controversy as plant geneticists' preference for a network of regional centres was rejected as too ambitious. The IBPGR was created as a centralized institute in the image of the other Green Revolution institutes, with the Northern-dominated group of financial donors firmly in control. Under this regime plant genetic resources have been collected more or less freely from around the world as the common heritage of humankind, and effectively appropriated by the institute concerned without any political oversight by the international community or by the Third World countries which donated the genetic material in the first place. Worse, property rights are often slapped onto the new varieties developed by Northern companies from material from developing countries, while farmers' efforts in developing and maintaining genetic diversity go unrewarded. These problems and others have led to fierce battles in the UN Food and Agriculture Organization (FAO) and other international fora as the Third World has attempted to wrest back some control overs its natural resources.

Signs of hope in a changing world?

Over recent years there has been a rediscovery of the role of small-scale agriculture as a cornerstone of development. It is now increasingly recognized that indigenous farming systems based on mixed cropping, soil and water conservation, and biological pest management not only conserve and utilize a tremendous mosaic of genetic diversity, but can produce more output and a wider range of harvested products, particularly in marginal environments. The recognition that farmers can and do play a crucial role in the conservation and management of genetic and other natural resources has largely coincided with a call for environmentally sustainable development which conventional, Western-based models of agriculture are increasingly being seen as unable to provide. After decades of neglect by official circles, the knowledge of farmers and their innovative capacity is coming to be seen by policy makers as the key to sustainable agriculture.

The international community recognized the importance of small farmers in development when, following the UN World Food Conference in 1974, it set up the International Fund for Agricultural Development to provide credit to small farmers on concessional terms. More recently the FAO has rejuvenated its approach to agricultural development under the new banner of 'sustainable agriculture and rural development' (SARD). At the same time, the last few years have seen a growing consensus over the particular issues of plant genetic resources. Following heated debates in the FAO, a Global System for Plant Genetic Resources is being put together. This recognizes farmers' rights 'arising from the past, present and future contributions of farmers in conserving, improving, and making available plant genetic resources'. (Resolution adopted at FAO Conference, November 1989, Rome.) More recent agreements have been largely catalysed by the Keystone Dialogue (Box 1.1), which has brought togther protagonists from government, industry and NGOs to work out a better international genetic resources order in their common interests. Its proposals, which will be presented to the UN's 1992 Earth Summit, give a very strong recognition of the role of farmers and their organizations in conserving and sustainably utilizing genetic resources at the grassroots level.

While these are positive trends, major obstacles remain. Genetic resources considerations are still not integrated into the activities of the mainstream development agencies, whether they be multilateral, bilateral or non-governmental; likewise international policies on trade, aid and finance tend to ignore the impact on genetic diversity and on the role of small-scale farmers in conservation and development; and most of the responses of the formal plant breeding and agricultural research system are still limited to policy statements, while the overall tendency in most countries is to continue to promote systems based on monoculture. There are, in addition, many new and dangerous trends: in particular, the new challenges from biotechnology which, coupled with the continuing privatization of genetic resources through patenting, threaten to scupper the advances achieved to date.

Farmers: growing diversity

The role of farmers may have been neglected by the formal system over the past decades but farmers have been far from inactive in developing alternatives and pressing for change. Their organizations have been cultivating, conserving and fieldwork. Such work needs to be recognized, rewarded and strengthened.

The linkage between the formal and informal innovation systems in plant breeding is a continuous and dynamic one. For strengthening the role of local communities in the conservation and improvement of landraces, it will be desirable that agricultural universities, research institutes and extension agencies provide training and technical support to farmers' associations and communities and undertake participatory research with them.

Community-level work is chronically underfunded. Genetic losses could be prevented in these programmes through provision of modest funding tied to specific conservation/utilization objectives.

In fashioning our solutions, our sense of urgency has helped us to overcome many of the significant differences of viewpoint represented among the participants. Outside observers would have thought this impossible a few years ago. In honesty, we ourselves had doubts that we could reach substantial agreement. We hope that the consensus we have achieved lends power to our message and our recommendations.'

developing traditional plant varieties, sometimes in areas out of the reach of the Green Revolution, sometimes in direct opposition to it. As described earlier, farmers have traditionally developed and maintained a diversity of crops and varieties in their farming systems. More recently, farmers' groups and other organizations working with farmers have been engaged in a range of activities to meet the challenges of present-day conditions, attempting to counter the negative effects of official policy and employing new technologies and the help of formal institutions in order to improve and build upon their farmer-based systems. New initiatives and ways of working are frequently demanded because the environment in which farmers find themselves has changed. To a large extent written by people who work closely with farmers and their communities, this book presents experiences of what is being done at the local level to conserve some of the genetic heritage on which all of us depend.

With the continuing onslaught of uniform new varieties being pushed by many national institutions and international aid agencies and research services, farmer-based organizations are playing an important role in rescuing traditional varieties through collection exercises; Chapters 2 and 4 give examples of activities of this kind. The varieties which are collected are distributed amongst other farmers or stored in community or official genebanks. These types of activities are usually the initiative of small-farmer based NGOs, but Chapter 8 provides an example of a governmental genebank service playing a catalytic and crucial role. While most of the examples given in this book deal with important agricultural crops, Kihika Kiambi and Monica Opole (Chapter 6) describe how traditional trees, used for fuel, fodder, timber and many other purposes, as well as traditional vegetables and medicinal plants, are collected in this way and then made available to farmers and the wider public through community organizations.

Many of the authors describe the importance of local seed stores in ensuring the availability of local varieties for farmers' use. These community seedbanks help to strengthen local control over genetic resources. This concept has been built upon in a number of ways. Andrea Gaifami (Chapter 9) explains the rationale for establishing a locally controlled semi-commercial seed company to put seed supply on a firm economic footing. Melaku Worede (Chapter 8) describes how the state-run genetic resources programme in Ethiopia links community seedbanks with the national genebank, so facilitating the availability of a wider range of genetic material to farmers, in addition to providing technical support.

One way to stimulate conservation of traditional plant varieties is to improve their agronomic performance, thereby increasing the incentives for keeping them. Since farmers are continually improving their varieties by mass selection, most of the experiences include this activity in some way. But on-farm selection and breeding is taken a stage further by the MASIPAG programme described in Chapter 2. In this programme the specific expertise of scientists is combined with the knowledge of farmers to produce improved varieties based mostly, but not wholly, on local genetic materials. Similarly in Ethiopia (Chapter 8), specialized plant-breeding techniques are made available to farmers to improve and maintain their traditional varieties. These are both examples of how the traditional practices and knowledge of farmers can be sustained and built upon by more formal scientific expertise.

Andrew Mushita describes a project to promote the use (and therefore the conservation) of local varieties of the small-grained cereals sorghum and millet (Chapter 9). Technically, the components of this farmer-based system mirror those of the formal system: collecting, multiplication, breeding, exchange, storage. One major difference is the active participation of farmers; selection and conservation activities are decentralized to the community level, giving farmers control over their local genetic resources. The other major difference of this and other farmer-based programmes is that conservation and use are integrated. This can be very efficient since there is continued adaptation of varieties to changing agronomic and socio-economic needs.

As one of the major problems facing the informal system is the loss of local knowledge, an important activity of NGOs is to reverse this trend. Sometimes this means countering the official propaganda which denigrates traditional practices; this is one of the aim's of Swissaid's work (Chapter 11). As in the case of Kenya (Chapter 6), this entails reversing long-established trends to devalue traditional knowledge. Sometimes it means passing on knowledge to a wider group through education and training programmes. To this end, changing public opinion and awareness-raising is crucial. Related to these grassroots practical activities, peoples' organizations, North and South, have been campaigning for recognition and support for farmer-based systems. Many of the NGOs involved in practical support work exchange information and experiences, organize workshops, and come together for joint lobbying activities and dialogue with the formal system.

This book gives a sample of the wide range of experiences in practical, farmer-based conservation and use of plant genetic resources. Generally, the experiences of farmer-based groups illustrate the resilience of their systems, despite the fact that the formal system of research institutes, genebanks and plant breeders has tended to work against those systems. Nevertheless, some of the changes which have occurred as a result of official policies have weakened traditional conservation mechanisms, through erosion of cultural systems or of genetic diversity itself; in addition,

11

increasing demands are being placed on farming systems, whether due to rural population growth, the needs of an expanding urban population or other forces outside the control of small-scale farmers. All of the contributions in this book stress that the time has come not only to recognize that farmers can and do conserve, use and improve plant genetic resources effectively, but that this approach should be supported by the formal system rather than impeded by it.

A way forward

The openings for a better system to conserve and develop genetic resources described earlier are encouraging, but need desperately to be translated into practice. There are at least three levels which should be addressed:

○ the full range of policies which impinge on agricultural development should be reassessed for its effects on plant genetic resources and farmers' ability to manage them; where necessary, such policies should be adjusted;
○ the current priorities for research and development should make farmers the starting point of research;
○ the informal sector (that is, farmers, their associations and the NGOs working with them) should be provided with the resources and tools to strengthen its own form of innovation in genetic conservation and breeding.

Resetting the policies

More often than not, current policies, in both the North and the South, are set against agricultural production rather than for it. Many governments and international financing agencies see agricultural activities as subservient to more prestigious industrial projects; they promote low prices for agricultural products and dictate policies to the detriment of small farmers. In many developing countries, it is cheaper to rely on aid or on the collapsed world market for food than it is to develop agricultural production. Many credit schemes and market forces act against local farming communities and the diversity they are maintaining. National economic policies are currently under scrutiny in many developing countries as the International Monetary Fund (IMF) and the World Bank promote their 'structural adjustment programmes' (SAPs). But these market-oriented approaches often exacerbate the destructive trends already present by pushing for export crops rather than food production, the opening of local markets to the international grain trade rather the promotion of food security, and for the privatization of seed companies which are unlikely to meet small farmers' needs. All of these harmful policies must be reversed, urgently.

Restructuring the research
Some of the experiences presented in this book illustrate what can be achieved when science and the formal system are turned to work with farmers (in particular, see Chapter 2 on the MASIPAG programme and Chapter 8 on the work of the Ethiopian genebank). Scientists from research institutes must understand that farmers have been conserving and breeding plants far longer than they have; farmers usually know what is threatened by genetic erosion, often much better than scientists. They tend to know which plants are useful for what purposes and where the wild species are. But most of all, farmers know what they need and how they can improve their systems. If we do not listen to them, we will fail to promote viable agricultural development strategies. In the penultimate chapter, Pat Mooney calls for a radical reorientation of the formal system so that it serves farmers in their breeding and conservation work.

The IARCs were the main protagonists of the Green Revolution and they should now play a major role in reorienting agricultural research so that it serves the needs of farmers. The system must be turned upside down so that farmers are considered full and equal partners in research rather than the target for end products. There have already been some examples of participatory plant-breeding approaches in the IARCs themselves, notably with the breeding of legumes to insect resistance at the International Crops Research Institute for the Semi-Arid Tropics (ICRISAT) in India, bean-breeding programmes at the International Centre for Tropical Agriculture (CIAT) in Colombia, and potato-breeding programmes at the International Potato Centre (CIP) in Peru. But these are isolated examples.

The structure of the IARCs should also be reformed, and they should be made accountable to a UN body. The focus of many centres on particular crops has helped them to escape the political realities of the effects of their technology on local people and environments; it is also a major obstacle to providing anything relevant for small farmers in marginal areas, where the point is often not so much the increase of singular crop yields but rather the improvement of the farming systems as a whole. The structure and operations of most of the IARCs should be decentralized, with research moving away from work on isolated crops to focus on those specific farming systems important to a particular region. This should have a profound effect on research activities at the national level. In many countries, the IARCs are seen by the formal research service as prestigious models worthy of imitation and, indeed, many national programmes are currently acting like IARC subsidiaries. By restructuring towards complex farming systems, where farmers are the first element, the decentralized, regionalized and participatory IARC system could have a major influence on reforming and strengthening national programmes.

Strengthening the informal sector
While governments and the scientists from the formal sector should redesign formal research structures, it is crucial also that they support the work of farmers in innovation at the grassroots level, where community organizations and NGOs, including the donor agencies, have a critical role to play. The experiences of farmer-based groups throughout the Third World point to common contraints: the lack of long-term funding for what is by nature long-term work; the lack of adapted techniques and methodologies for grassroots conservation activites; the lack of trained personnel to participate in local-level work; lack of support from the formal sector; and adverse policies which undermine what farmers are trying to achieve.

Development agencies can help out through financial and political support, which means providing the necessary resources to carry out the work. This support remains desperately needed. It is often critical for the success of local initiatives. Genetic resources activities can go from setting up simple community seed banks to broader-scale regional projects involving collection, identification, multiplication, maintenance and evaluation. To that must be added breeding, which can, again, go from the most simple mass selection techniques to more complex crossing experiments. Finally, seed production and marketing of improved local cultivars is necessary to get adequate quantities of good seed distributed to farmers in time.

Aside from supporting specific genetic resources-related projects, the development agencies can play a vital role by integrating concerns for genetic diversity into all of their rural development projects. They can evaluate the genetic-resources 'friendliness' of their projects, often in collaboration with local groups; in the name of aid or emergency relief, development agencies frequently contribute unwillingly to the destruction of local genetic diversity. Sometimes small-scale seed production projects can also ignore the importance of using local diversity and preserving it in the process. Just as potential projects are evaluated for their impact on the environment in general or for gender equity, genetic diversity issues should be considered for all projects. Genetic resources are a very powerful tool for sustainable development if this is recognized and approached openly.

Putting farmers' rights into practice

All of this should lead the discussions on farmers' rights now held at the international level beyond a mere recognition of the role of farmers in the maintenance and improvement of plant genetic resources. Farmers' rights have been formally recognized by the international community but still lack implementation. The concept must give rise to concrete mechanisms, legal, financial and technical, to ensure that farmers can actually take up their rights. Reasserting ownership over seeds is not so much the point if farmers are not in a position to further develop them. To be meaningful, farmers' rights must result in: capacity-building at the grassroots level, providing local communities with their own tools to improve stable, low-input production systems; the reorientation of national and international agricultural research to better suit small-scale farmers' needs; and substantial new funding for farmer-based initiatives.

There is little hope for sound management of the world's genetic resources if the current biases toward élitist, technically isolated genebanks and top-down monoculture approaches to agricultural 'development' are merely reinforced. Conservation and innovation in the field of genetic resources must be broadened. What stands out from the survey of farmer-based experiences presented in this book is the wide range of approaches. As many contributors argue, a diversity of techniques is required to guarantee the maintenance and development of genetic diversity itself. This must include the provision of the mechanisms to strengthen innovation and conservation at the grassroots level as well as correcting the problems of national and international agricultural research strategies. Then small farmers, the backbone of so many societies, will have a real opportunity to move forward and improve food production systems with a long-term perspective.

2 Community plant genetic resources management: experiences in Southeast Asia

RENE SALAZAR*

The widespread use of few genetically uniform high-yielding rice varieties is decimating Southeast Asia's wealth of locally adapted landraces. It is also undermining social structures and ecological balances and increasing poverty among small farmers. Southeast Asian NGOs, in co-operation with farmers' organizations and progressive scientists, are starting to collect and conserve traditional varieties to strengthen farmer-based breeding programmes for low-input agriculture. The first results are promising, but it will be difficult to move further without the proper support.

On 14 November 1990, a group of NGO participants to a Southeast Asian training workshop on community seeds conservation visited a small village called Tap Klay, in Uthai Thani province, near the Burmese border of West Thailand. The village belongs to the Karen hill tribe people living in the area. Among the crops found in one farmer's field were five traditional rice varieties. While talking with the Karen farmer, the group discovered that he had decided he would replace those rice cultivars with mulberry trees during the next planting season. That way, he could get crop loans and insurance offered by the Thai government. The oldest member of the Karen village remembered that those rices had always been with the tribe. He remembered vaguely that two of them were brought by his grandparents from Laos, because they were particularly good for children. But the government's mulberry tree promotion programme was just too good to refuse.

---

* Rene Salazar is from the Philippines. He has been working with NGOs on community organization and grassroots conservation strategies at the national and regional levels for some ten years. Rene is currently the Seeds Programme Coordinator for the Southeast Asia Regional Institute for Community Education (SEARICE), based in Manila. He is part of the steering committee of the Asian Seeds for Survival Programme.

In East Java, Indonesian NGOs reported some time ago that local government officials had burned down the traditional rice cultivars planted by the farmers. In 1984, the same incidents were reported by another NGO in Central Java. Top government officials of Indonesia explained in one conference that it is the policy of their government to achieve rice sufficiency through high productivity, and that all rice lands which benefit from government irrigation programmes and other agricultural infrastructures are 'discouraged' from planting rice varieties not approved by the Ministry of Agriculture.

In the Mekong Delta of South Vietnam, the modern rice 'high-yielding varieties' (HYVs) have displaced the original cultivars. Together, the Mekong Basin and Delta form Southeast Asia's centre of rice genetic diversity. The Vietnamese government's programme of increasing rice production for export is anchored on an aggressive drive to introduce rice HYVs into the paddy fields. Coupled with structural and agricultural policy reforms, rice production in the Delta increased initially, and was the main source of Vietnamese rice exports for the last two years. However, sustainability of this agricultural development strategy is in serious doubt. This year, 1991, all over the nine Mekong Delta provinces, billboards of chemical pesticides adorn the roads, an unknown sight barely two years ago. As in other countries which took on the Green Revolution varieties, the genetic uniformity of the new rice seeds is again requiring blanket applications of chemicals in order to survive. And for the first time in the history of rice cultivation in Vietnam, the country is now faced with a massive invasion of brown plant hoppers and tungro infestations, much more serious than earlier attacks.

Before the introduction of rice HYVs, the Philippines may have had several thousands of local rice cultivars. But at present, only a few hundred upland traditional cultivars are left in the fields. While several thousand Filipino landraces are kept within the massive International Rice Research Institute (IRRI) genebank, we can confidently assume that very little or no rice collecting has been done in places which are far from the main roads, or in areas of continuing civil strife. Yet, over the years, even many of these harder-to-reach areas have become exposed to the introduction of genetically uniform HYVs, displacing the old cultivars forever.

Changing lifestyles and social systems, perverse financial incentives, the use of force, coercion or intimidation . . . they all have the same devastating effect: the diversity of plant genetic resources in the farmers' fields is being destroyed throughout Southeast Asia, and farmers are losing control over the most vital link in agricultural production, the seeds. These changes have had serious agronomic, economic and cultural repercussions for local farming communities. But alternative approaches to genetic resources conservation and use, based on farmers' own innovations and the support of community-based organizations, are starting to get into motion.

The impacts of genetic erosion

Genetic erosion undermines food security and contributes to the powerlessness of farmers throughout the Third World. 'Miracle rice', the first major product of Philippines-based IRRI, was hastily disseminated to farmers throughout Southeast Asia with little regard for its long-term effects on their livelihoods. In 1966, IRRI released the first semi-dwarf HYV rice, IR-8. It soon dominated rice production in tropical Asia. While it could yield well in a broad range of climates, it required heavy doses of fertilizer and turned out to be highly susceptible to pests and disease, which gave rise to unprecedented epidemics. A few years later, IRRI released IR-36, which was said to be more resistant. By 1982, it covered 11 million hectares of the 150 million devoted to rice in Asia. In some countries, like the Philippines, Indonesia and Vietnam, the lone variety IR-36 represented 60 per cent of all rice production. How many well-adapted landraces did these superstars wipe out? Who calculated the long-term costs to farmers of these vulnerable monocultures?

Some of the effects of the HYV technology were summed up in a recent report issued by the MASIPAG programme (*Mga Magsasaka at Siyentipiko para sa Pagpapaunlad ng Agham Pang-agrikultura,* or 'Farmer-Scientist Participation for Development'), which brings together farmers, scientists and NGOs to conserve traditional rice in the Philippines:

After more than 20 years of adopting the HYV technology, the farmers and the country as a whole experienced only small, misleading nominal gains. The country, despite its HYVs,

19

continues to import rice. The gains which were experienced during the early years of adopting the HYVs turned into an accumulated burden for farmers and the country's economy as well. Farmer-borrowers were not able to repay their agricultural loans, and remain among the most impoverished sector of society. Indeed, not only were production goals not met, but society also starts to reap the ill-effects of an unsound technology in its ecological environment.

A study made by the Nutrition Centre of the Philippines in 1980 showed that the nutritional status of the children in the central plains of Luzon, the leading rice-growing area of the Philippines, actually deteriorated at the time when rice harvests were increasing. This may be due in part to the loss of traditional sources of protein which came from the paddy fields of Southeast Asia. With the introduction of HYV seeds and their chemical packages, turtles, frogs, shrimp, shellfish and birds, which were part of local diets, disappeared or were poisoned by toxic pesticides.

Farming communities are also disrupted culturally by the loss of traditional cultivars. Harvesting, weeding, threshing and hulling of local landraces traditionally provide employment for a lot of women and children. But the semi-dwarf HYVs are harvested with sickles, rather than with small hand knives, and this effectively excludes women from the harvest. An Indonesian NGO survey released last year showed that the 200 or more women harvesting each hectare of rice in 1970 were replaced by just 10 or 20 men in 1990. Women's labour was also dislocated by the use of chemical herbicides.

The productive activity of the less fit and the weaker members of the community was also affected by the introduction of HYVs. Old people, widows, children and semi-invalids, who had roles in agriculture production before, are now considered burdens to the farming community. Yet the increased incidence of poverty amongst farming communities is not usually taken into the balance sheet when the (doubtful) successes of HYVs are presented.

The informal and the formal conservation systems

Farming communities all over the world, and throughout the ages, have provided us with the crop genetic diversity we have today. Through domestication and selection, the diversity of crops adapted to a full range of different conditions and needs has been created: IRRI has collected more than 85,000 accessions of rice, mostly from Asia; the Vedic literature of India talks of more than half a million rice cultivars; in Thailand and in Vietnam, excavations of ancient ruins and graves dating from three to six thousand years ago have produced earthen pots containing rice seeds. Therefore, when we talk about plant genetic resources and their conservation, we are talking about the genius and efforts of thousands of years of farming generations in the South. When these genetic resources are displaced from farmers' fields, we are losing this inheritance forever.

We consider those plant genetic resources conservation activities initiated by governments, research institutions, universities and scientists as composing the formal system. The informal system, on the other hand, consists of those initiatives developed and led by farmers, which include their traditional practices from the past, their conservation work carried out in marginal areas and their collective efforts to recover crop genetic diversity and control over farming systems. This is sometimes done in collaboration with NGOs or with progressive scientists.

These two systems can and should be complementary. But in the past two or three decades, the world has focused its reliance on the formal system, while totally ignoring the informal system. This has very serious consequences: first of all, we cannot rely solely on a system which is fairly new, relative to the proven capacity of farmer communities to conserve such resources for thousands of years; second, the idea of static conservation in genebanks is not ideal; the seeds may not be viable when planted under conditions which will prevail 20 or 30 years from now. There are also a number of practical and logistical problems with a centralized approach.

Collections made by the formal system tend to be limited to areas which are easily accessible, such as those near roads. Farmers, on the other hand, are wherever the resources are. Examples of inadequate rice-collecting systems are the cases of Vietnam and Mozambique. Due to the war, only a few hundred rice cultivars of Vietnamese rice, reportedly 650 accessions, were collected by IRRI. This is an area which is a major centre of rice genetic diversity! In Mozambique, transport across the Indian Ocean allowed the introduction of *indica* rice from Asia several hundred years ago. Yet is is reported that there are only two rice accessions indigenous to Mozambique in the IRRI genebank.

The collectors of the formal system also have limited time. At least three months must be spent in one specific area to capture the genetic variation of local rice crops. In Cambodia, for example, the rice harvest runs from October, for the early-maturing cultivars, until January, for the late-maturing ones. In practice, is almost impossible for the formal sector scientists to collect all this diversity of the various rices. The Khmer farmer, on the other hand, is there all the time. She or he knows what is under threat and what is not, where it is and what it is useful for.

The farmers also know best which genetic characteristics they need. Sometimes, for them, productivity measured in kilograms per hectare may be relegated to second or even fourth priority. And as the farmers are in constant interaction with their environment, the conservation and selection of genetic resources is dynamic. What the farmers continue to plant, select and use will continue to co-evolve with the changing environment. Their keen observation and selection activities will continue to improve and provide genetic traits which are valuable to their needs, and often to those of the world.

Farmers as innovators

In marginal lands, where the uniform and ideal production conditions required by the genetically uniform HYV seeds are not possible, farming communities continue to conserve and improve their plant genetic resources. The genepool of upland rice cultivars in the Philippines, for example, has generally withstood displacement. A recent NGO survey and sampling of traditional rice cultivars in five sites on the island of Mindanao resulted in the collection of around 123 traditional cultivars, 104 of which were from the uplands.

But even in the well-irrigated lands suitable for HYVs, farmers continue to innovate. For example, in the province of Cotabato in Mindanao, a farmer in the town of Santa Catalina discovered, amongst his land planted to the IRRI variety IR-36, that some rice plants had managed to survive heavy flooding. It was even possible, he said, that the rice plants came with the flood and not his tranplsanted seeds.

When the rice matured, the farmer collected and planted the seeds again, keenly observing their agronomic performance. After several generations of careful selection, the farmer stabilized a new population. He called it Bordagol (short, solid and strong). Bordagol's palatability is remarkable. The taste is completely distinct from any variety currently available in the country and it commands a high price in the markets of the provinces of Cotabato.

While Bordagol's yield per hectare is 20 per cent lower than that of current HYVs, it is stable and productive with only half the chemical fertilizer input; it tillers well (grows shoots), outgrowing the weeds so that weeding or the use of herbicides is not required; and it is less susceptible to pest infestations and has the same maturing characteristics as IR-36. It has become a popular variety planted in the three provinces of Cotabato and in two other provinces of Mindanao. Progressive agricultural scientists are now studying the plant. Clearly, what came out of one farmer's field is comparable in quality to the output of giant research institutes and represents an important contribution to the local economy. But the formal sector has difficulty in recognizing this.

As the price of chemical inputs continues to rise, the need for traditional, low-input varieties is increasing. Some farming communities are responding to meet the new demand. One village in North Cotabato, called barrio Batasan, in co-operation with a church youth organization, developed a three-hectare seed farm to produce planting materials of traditional cultivars for farmers in the surrounding villages. Together, they dug almost three kilometres of irrigation canal. For its first year in 1990, the farm, supported by the Swiss NGO HEKS, produced and distributed locally adapted maize seeds of a variety called Tinigib which is popular among non-rice-eating peoples. Aside from their principal activity in maize seed, traditional cultivars of vegetable seeds are also produced, and the seed farm aims to expand into traditional rice seed production in 1991 or 1992.

In Au Giang province of the Mekong Delta in Vietnam, farming communities continue to plant a traditional variety called Moc Bui. Under the ideal conditions demanded by HYVs, Moc Bui produces an average of eight tonnes per hectare. No weeding or herbicide is required and, as a medium-height variety, it returns more straw to the land. Moc Bui is popular among the farmers in the Mekong areas.

Through careful selection, the farmers have developed a Moc Bui cultivar which is shorter by an average of 17 centimetres for areas where water can be controlled more easily. At the Phrey Phdau rice station in Cambodia, a rice germplasm collection and improvement programme was conducted with support from Oxfam-Belgique and Oxfam-USA. The Phrey Phdau rice station has a collection of 1,320 local rice cultivars, all of which are fully characterized. After cleaning and selection, the station has released '2 Somrung 2', a local cultivar which proved to be very reliable, producing an average of five tonnes per hectare under low input conditions. The Phrey Phdau rice station has also conducted experiments to compare the agronomic performances of one traditional rice cultivar with the HYV IR-42 under a range of conditions. The results showed that the two rice cultivars performed equally well. A research report compiled by Xavier Cornet of Oxfam-Belgique stated that

> There was . . . no comparative difference in the average yield between the two varieties, IR-42 and the local 'Prambei Kuor'. A traditional mid-season variety like Prambei Kuor, even if planted relatively late, can thus be integrated with the same efficiency as medium-cycle modern varieties like IR-42 in a cropping pattern including a green manured crop. The ability of the traditional variety for delayed transplanting could be regarded as an advantage. . . . Beyond the comparable yields obtained, the superior rice straw production and grain quality of Prambei Kuor also are to be taken into account.

In Thailand, a local NGO, Technology for Rural and Ecological Enrichment (TREE), began a rescue operation to save plant genetic resources from being lost as the Thai government aggressively introduced new seeds coupled with agricultural loans and extension services. After two years, TREE was able to collect over 4,000 accessions of rice, and almost 3,000 samples of other food crops. Pending the establishment of community seed banks, duplicates of these collections are currently stored at the government's National Rice Germplasm Bank. This illustrates how the informal and the formal systems can co-operate beneficially.

There are numerous other examples of the value and importance of traditional varieties when they are conserved and used at the local level. Thirty kilometres from the capital town of Roxas on the island of Panay in Central Philippines, the BINHI Agricultural Foundation was able to select and clean a traditional rice cultivar which performed well under low input conditions. In a village in Klaten, Central Java, Indonesia, farmers collected 26 traditional rice cultivars. The farmers observed their performance compared to that of the HYVs promoted by the government and found that, in the absence of chemical inputs, seven traditional cultivars outperformed three HYVs. In the village of Tegalsari, also in Klaten, another farmer community, working with Didi Soetomo, had 37 rice cultivars from the areas stored in its community seed bank. Two of these out-performed the rice HYVs distributed by the government. The same community seed bank project has mass-distributed two chili cultivars to local farmers.

MASIPAG: farmers and scientists for development

In the Philippines, a community group established the alternative plant breeding programme, MASIPAG, in co-operation with progressive scientists from the University of the Philippines at Los Baños, in 1986. MASIPAG is designed for rice lands that have lost much of their genetic diversity over the last 20 years. It has the following aims:

○ to develop improved varieties which require low external inputs but have comparatively reasonable yields, by utilizing selected traditional varieties which are resistant to adverse climatic conditions, pests and diseases;
○ to encourage farmers' participation in the actual breeding work, nursery management, evaluation and selection of the varieties, so that they produce their own seeds according to their own perceived needs and resources;
○ to enable the farmers to gain control of their seeds and the promising lines by allowing them to select their own parental stocks;
○ to establish farmers' seed banks to help reduce genetic erosion; and
○ to simplify the process of selection and dissemination of the promising new crosses.

The MASIPAG programme collected around 210 accessions, most of which were contributions from farmer organizations all over the country. One hundred and twenty-seven of these were traditional cultivars, while 83 were improved

25

varieties. They were all tested at the programme research station with farmers' direct participation. A total of 100 cross-combinations were made over a three-year period. Of the 71 crosses made in the first and second years, only 30 remained from the 1990 dry season, yielding 101 selected lines. One half of these showed a potential to produce good yields and disease resistance under low input conditions. The third breeding effort in the 1989 wet season yielded 28 cross-combinations and 1.24 kilograms of second generation (F2) seed in the 1990 dry season harvest. The most significant aspect of this was the farmers' preference for traditional varieties, rather than the improved ones, to serve as parental material in the breeding programme.

Seed distribution started from the first and second crops planted in the original sites in Nueva Ecija where the initial collection of 47 cultivars was planted by the members of the farmer organizations in the 1986 wet season and in the 1987 dry season. So far, the project seed collections have reached 19 provinces nationwide, and a total of 40,000 kilos of seed selections from 34 cultivars has been distributed by the central station and its satellites.

The first experiments in the 1988 wet season showed that without chemical fertilizers and pesticides, traditional varieties could yield as much as or more than the improved cultivars, including HYVs. The grain yields ranged from 3.7 to 5.7 tonnes per hectare for five traditional varieties, compared to 3.5 to 5.2 tonnes for six improved varieties, and 3.2 to 5.2 for two HYVs. In the 1989 wet season, the average of the six traditional varieties planted produced 3.98 tonnes per hectare while the improved varieties produced 3.87 tonnes.

The bottlenecks to community conservation

A major problem facing many community plant genetic resources conservation schemes is adverse government policy. Most national policies in Southeast Asia are not only not favourable to such schemes; in some cases governments actively discourage plant genetic resources conservation. The Indonesian cases cited earlier are of the extreme type. Perverse economic and financial incentives are equally effective in harming local varieties. Extension services, crop loans and insurance allotted to farmers, often on the condition that they use new HYVs, have caused a lot of damage. The comparatively good initial performances of new HYVs upon their introduction, coupled with heavily subsidized production costs, have encouraged farmers to discard many of their old cultivars.

There is a severe lack of scientific support for community-based systems. In consequence, development of appropriate systems and instruments that can be used at the community level has lagged behind. One of the reasons for the lack of scientific support for farmer-based germplasm conservation is that it conflicts with the narrow career interests of some scientists. Some agricultural scientists in the Philippines are lobbying hard to pass a law allowing the patenting of altered and discovered germplasm, a move which threatens to deny the rights of farmers over valuable germplasm which they might help to identify.

Economic and financial difficulties add to the constraints against farmers. Farmers cannot afford to be curators of traditional seeds for all of humanity without corresponding support, and the tendency is to leave behind local cultivars that no longer fit a present socio-economic condition. The cost of their loss for the unpredictable future is incalculable.

There is a gross lack of financial resources for grassroots projects. Reflecting the general lack of recognition of farmers' contributions to the present richness of the world's genetic diversity is the lack of resources available to farming communities to conserve and improve their planting materials. Farmers' fields should not be downgraded to one-time collecting areas for high-tech genebanks but recognized as areas of on-going conservation and crop improvement. Financial support should be made available in respect of this. As far as we are concerned, we do not know of any farming community in all of Southeast Asia being directly supported by the formal system to conserve and improve its planting materials. Whatever support farming communities receive comes from NGOs, and is too small to make a large impact. For example, a survey and collection of surviving traditional rice cultivars of the island of Mindanao undertaken by a farmers' organization had a total budget of only US$15,000. This should be compared to IRRI's budget ($31 million) and the relative effectiveness of each evaluated.

Previously, the lack of external support and new techniques adapted to community plant germplasm conservation was not a common concern. Conservation and improvement through selection was part of farming life. The knowledge related to plant resources which farmers developed was part of the general knowledge of the community; it was handed down from generation to generation and among peoples. But farmers are now suffering from rapidly changing agro-ecological conditions. Forests have been denuded, rainfall patterns have been altered, farm soils have been heavily subjected to chemical fertilizers, and pests and diseases have evolved into more virulent strains. All this puts a tremendous strain on farming communities and on their traditional cultivars and systems. Today, we are talking of plant genetic resources conservation under highly stressful conditions, and we are also seeing farmer communities trying to conserve resources not only from their own communities but also from outside their villages.

Improved and adapted techniques are required urgently. The volume of germplasm which a community of farmers who have decided to conserve seeds for their own and for other small farmers needs is much higher than what is traditionally within their capacities. There is simply not enough space, for example, above the cooking area in the kitchen where seeds are commonly kept. Good seed storage techniques are vital. Practices such as those of Asian villagers where larger seeds, particularly leguminous crops like soya, are kept in earthen jars with ash and charcoal, need to be assessed and improved.

Better and more appropriate documentation systems, adapted descriptor lists and simple conservation techniques amenable to farmers' control must be developed. Serious attention also needs to be given to the problem of the selective tendency of germplasm conservation. Farmers traditionally select the best seeds on the farm and some potentially useful characteristics may be missed. This method cannot claim to collect the fullest diversity possibly present on one farm. The same problem occurs when collecting for a community seed bank. Farmers tend to collect only what they perceive as the best. There is a need to balance the aims of conserving diversity with the farmer's need for next season's seeds and the socio-economic demands of the wider community.

The integrity of germplasm collections is threatened where, through lack of resources or other problems, the maintenance and propagation of collected landraces have to take place in agro-ecological conditions which may be significantly different from those from where the germplasm was collected. In the Philippine MASIPAG programme, for example, rice germplasm donated by farmers' associations all over the Philippines was regenerated and characterized at MASIPAG's main research station in Central Luzon. This is far from ideal.

It is clear that farmers hold a vast wealth of technological knowledge useful for the conservation and improvement of plant genetic resources. The perverse policies of some governments and international agencies which restrict farmers' traditional activities in seeds and promote genetic erosion must be abandoned. But that is not enough. Today's peasant farmers are under considerable strain to meet an increasing demand for food under conditions of a deteriorating environment. Concrete support – financial, scientific and technical – is required to enable farmers to continue to conserve and develop traditional and new varieties of plants.

3 Sowing community seed banks in Indonesia

DIDI SOETOMO*

The sustainability and diversity once characteristic of Indonesian agriculture are going rapidly downhill. Monocultures, chemicals and the government's narrow focus on rice have put farmers' security in peril throughout this agrarian country. Diversity and farmers' control over their own production systems must become the basis for true agricultural development. The community seed bank approach can be an important mechanism to facilitate conservation, training, networking and the diversification and improvement of farming systems.

Indonesia, covering almost two million square kilometres and lying on the equator, has a diverse wealth of natural resources, both biotic and abiotic: fertile soils, volcanic mountains, and tropical forests. It is an essentially agrarian country in which the majority live in the rural areas and more than 80 per cent of the people work in the agricultural sector. The cultivated area is divided among twelve million hectares of dry land and seven million hectares of paddy where rice is grown. The centre of rice cultivation is Java island, where the agricultural system is most advanced. Sixty per cent of Indonesia's population of 180 million lives in Java. Other islands, like Sulawesi, Kalimantan, Sumatra, Nusa Tenggara and Irian Jaya, still consist primarily of forest, with a rich diversity of plants, micro-organisms and animals.

Long before the modernization of agriculture along Western lines in the 1960s, Indonesian agriculture was sustainable and productive, particularly from an ecological point of view. Farmers used natural inputs, without chemicals, and a rich array of traditional landraces. Indonesia, for example,

* Didi Soetomo has been working with Indonesian NGOs concerned with education, rural development and ecology for more than 15 years. He is deeply concerned about genetic erosion caused by Green Revolution technologies, and its long-term effects on farmers' livelihoods. Over the past years, Didi has provided much inspiration and energy to strengthen the community seed bank movement in Indonesia.

has more than 13,000 indigenous landrace varieties of rice. Farmers were assured of a harvest every season and they practised multiple cropping. For fertilization, they used compost and manure from the livestock which they kept. The livestock also provided a workforce in the fields. This traditional system was fully sustainable with little genetic erosion, soil degradation or pollution.

But with the aim of reaching self-suffciency in rice production, the government has been implementing a programme of agricultural intensification. Through government schemes like BIMAS (the 'mass guidance programme', 1963) and its off-shoot INMAS (1967), farmers were provided with credit, seed, pesticides, chemical fertilizers and support for the cost of living. But after harvest, the farmers had to pay back all of these; in many cases they were unable to do so. In response to these problems, as of 1969 the government introduced new, yet more intensive, policies: INSUS and SUPRA INSUS, (or 'Intensification Technology Package). In these new package deals, farmers were encouraged to use chemicals to increase production, but production increases were a mere 2.3 per cent in 1984–5 and 1.8 per cent in 1985–6. In 1986, the yield increase was further down to 1 per cent, less than the increase in population. At that stage, Indonesia had to start importing rice from Thailand.

The whole package is dependent on high-tech, high-energy strategies. Farmers are forced to use chemical fertilizers, pesticides and irrigation. The high-yielding varieties (HYVs) need three times as much water as the traditional ones, according to the local farmers. To meet the demand for irrigation, the government constructed dams at Kedung Ombo, Gajah Mungkur and Mrica. Dam-building took many casualties in human lives, genetic resources and the natural landscape. People were forced out of Java and went to the forest areas where they cut down trees to build houses and cultivate the land.

Hybrid seed was introduced for several crops with the result that the farmers could no longer rely on seed they had selected and stored themselves, but were always dependent on the seed suppliers. Further, farmers were forced by official authorities to plant 20-hectare blocks of a single variety of rice. Except for those people in isolated villages who could continue to plant the indigenous varieties, farmers attempting to disregard these rules were intimidated by military and local government personnel. The economic and ecological results were disastrous. Economically, farmers could not keep up with the increased costs of production based on artificial fertilizer, pesticides and other inputs. Irrigation alone could cost 65 thousand rupiah (about US$33) per hectare every year, while farmers' incomes were not more than Rp135–270 thousand per year (US$67–135). At the same time, rice prices were kept low in order to buy political stability in the towns. Any crop failure, through disease, flooding or other natural disasters, could spell ruin for farmers.

The use of fertilizers had adverse ecological effects as populations of soil organisms were reduced. Pollution from pesticides increased, and the pesticides themselves became less effective as pests and diseases built up in the monoculture systems. In 1989, over 3,000 hectares of rice were threatened by tungro, locally known as Wereng disease. At the same time, 52,000 hectares were attacked by Sundep, a stem borer, in West Sumatra, and a further 70,000 hectares in West Java. Rice is the main staple for the people of Java, but in the other islands maize, cassava and the sago palm are very important. In the more isolated communities, people supplement their diet with a wide range of other foods. Government policy, through the SUPRA INSUS programme, has always been to promote the consumption of rice. People often assume that rice consumption implies a higher social status, that is to say that if you eat rice in Indonesia, you are considered 'more civilized'. But dependence on only one staple food can be highly dangerous, especially when its genetic base is narrow. The tragedy of the Irish potato famine in the last century illustrates this danger.

The community seed bank approach

'Java' means 'rice'. Most Indonesians live on this island, as farmers in the villages. They are the ones who feel the effects of genetic erosion most directly. Superficially, the Green Revolution increased rice yields, but in reality it was a disaster. Farmers became simply part of a food machine and social systems were undermined; women lost their jobs harvesting rice in the field. Farmers were no longer in control of their own lives.

While only big farmers and large corporations could

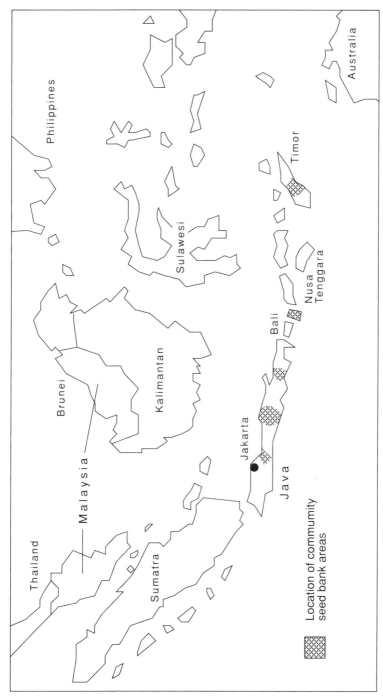

Figure 2. *The Indonesian archipelago showing the location of community seed bank projects in Java and nearby islands.*

Location of commumity
seed bank areas

benefit from the Green Revolution, all, but especially the small farmers, would benefit from an approach based on genetic diversity. But under current conditions it is not easy to develop genetic resource programmes at the local level. The government is hostile to the promotion of farming systems based on indigenous genetic resources. So for the farmers linking up with NGOs and sympathetic scientists is the only alternative. Good co-operation between them is essential, vital as it is to determine the principles, strategies and approaches to ensure efficient and effective programmes for sustainable agriculture.

The over-riding priority in Indonesian agriculture should be one of genetic security based on diversity. This would mean security for the farmer and, by using a wider range of genetic resources and avoiding monoculture, the use of chemicals, high-tech irrigation and mechanization can be avoided, with benefits for the environment. In Indonesia, and especially in Java, folk tradition holds that rice is not just a common plant but an incarnation of God. The local people always sow, look after and harvest their rice crops with the utmost care. At planting, they hold a ceremony in the fields and pray that their plants will flourish and produce a good harvest. Given the special role of rice in the lives of the people of Java, and the degree of genetic erosion which has already occurred, community seed bank programmes to conserve and develop genetic diversity in rice are especially important.

Farmers themselves should be involved in any seed bank programme from the beginning of the project right up to its evaluation. Such a participatory approach strengthens the security of genetic resource conservation: if all farmers are actually using plant varieties, it is safer than trying to keep them in a cold room in some far-off genebank. Additionally, a participatory approach has a built-in training and networking component, as farmers learn from each other.

To ensure the continuity of community-based projects, there is a need for institution-building and the training of facilitators who know and understand the communities with which they work. In this way it can be assured that the smaller and poorer farmers, who generally have farms of less than half a hectare, really benefit.

Indonesian NGOs became involved in genetic resources projects in 1984. In that year, in Klaten and in many other parts of the country, explosive outbreaks of plant diseases occurred. The impact on farmers was terrible, as they lost their rice harvests for about two years running. The main diseases were caused by brown rice hopper and a variety of virus attacks. All efforts to wipe out the diseases had been tried, all kinds of pesticides used, Rp100,000 had been spent out of the farmers' savings, but still they could not reap a decent harvest. The farmers became worried for their survival.

This is why indigenous varieties were experimented with. One field of 1,800 square metres was planted with the traditional variety Rojolele. This landrace had become very rare due to displacement by the HYVs, even on Klaten where, because of its delicious taste and fragrance, it was most popular. Production costs of Rojolele are well below those for the HYVs because there is no need to use pesticides or chemical fertilizers; neither are Rojolele plants attacked by the rice hoppers.

The success of the demonstration plot encouraged farmers to return to planting Rojolele. Seed was produced from the plot and lent to farmers, who returned a similar quantity after cropping. Table 3.1 compares the benefits of the traditional variety with those of the HYV IR-64.

The comparison shows that, despite the high potential yield of IR-64, farmers are better off growing Rojolele than the HYV, and many farmers are now changing back to the

Table 3.1: Rojolele landrace vs. IRRI's IR-64

Character	Rojolele	IR-64
Growing period	150 days	130 days
Water requirement	average	high
Weeding required	once	twice
Urea fertilizer rate	100 kg/ha	200 kg/ha
TCS rate[1]	80 kg/ha	150 kg/ha
Resistance to rats	average	low
Resistance to hopper	average	low
Resistance to birds	average	high
Yield	2 tonnes/ha	3 tonnes/ha
Net income to farmer[2]	Rp1,400,000	Rp1,200,000

[1] TCS rate measures response to fertilizer
[2] Rp2,000 = US$1

35

traditional varieties. Another benefit of the traditional variety is that farmers do not have to buy seed from external suppliers, as they do with IR-64, and this allows community seed banks to be developed. Local communities can then benefit further by marketing seeds themselves.

Community seed banks developed in Klaten usually involve between 10 and 20 farmers together covering four to eight hectares. Success there is encouraging other districts to develop similar programmes, for example, in Boyolali, Karanganyar, Sukoharjo (central Java) and Malang (east Java). Within each seed bank project there are income-generating schemes and training programmes on how to cultivate traditional varieties. Groups exchange seed and ideas. Multilocational trials are being carried out to detect adaptations to particular areas. Gradually, farmers learn more about the characteristics of each variety and its products; at the same time, the pros and cons of the Green Revolution and alternative approaches to diversify production systems are actively discussed.

Now, over 30 varieties from the Philippines have been collected. Not all have the particular advantages of Rojolele but all have potential to be developed. Besides rice, the community seed banks are testing several horticultural crops, like watermelon and chili. The local varieties of these are threatened with displacement by hybrids from Taiwan.

The main problem with developing community seed bank programmes is that the schemes are contrary to government policy. Official policy holds that conservation should not be managed by farmers but should be the responsibility of the government through genebanks, in Indonesia or in other countries. But in reality, genetic resources are inseparable from farmers' needs and farmers themselves are the key to determining whether there is erosion or conservation of genetic resources. Farmers know the importance of using genetic resources sustainably, which assures that conservation at the community level is part of improving farming systems.

It is difficult to co-operate with the Indonesian government and, although NGOs have had some contacts with the ministries of the environment and agriculture, contact remains peripheral and insubstantial. Where there has been co-operation, with the government providing counterpart funds to NGO projects, these funds have been frozen when the

NGOs encouraged farmers to plant the traditional varieties against official policy.

The role of young scientists in the community seed bank programmes has been limited, as most of them agree with government policy or have links with the multinational corporations. Another problem is that the Green Revolution approach has undermined the traditional links between farmers and their environments; farmers now care less about the environment. This is exacerbated by the use of harmful imported products with misleading advertising. With the loss of the traditional varieties, it often seems impossible to return to using them. But in fact, there are usually some landraces still present. For example, in Klaten district, only two HYVs are used (IR-64 and Cisadane), while three landraces remain, although they are rarely planted.

Entrusting genetic resource conservation to developed countries puts developing countries in a dangerous and artificially created situation of dependency. It is also unreliable, as the genebanks are vulnerable to breakdowns. To ensure world food security, an alternative approach is required, based on *in situ* conservation in the countries of origin. Developed-country NGOs can promote such an approach through advocacy at international institutions like the UN FAO and the UN Environment Programme (UNEP). Conservation of genetic resources must be freed from the control of the multinational corporations and government genebanks and returned to the farmers whose livelihoods depend directly upon them.

4 An integrated NGO approach in Thailand

DAY-CHA SIRIPATRA and
WITOON LIANCHAMROON*

Thailand is fast losing its important share of genetic diversity: the forests are disappearing and the farm lands are growing pale under the spread of uniform and chemical-dependent HYVs. Worse yet, the government, bent on yield statistics and catering to trans-national corporations (TNCs), is doing little to preserve the seeds Thai farmers will need to face their future and everything to pre-vent the farmers from organizing themselves. NGOs are trying to intervene and turn the course of erosion around, but they have only just begun.

Thailand is exceptionally rich in genetic diversity since it is situated within important Vavilov centres of diversity (see p. 4) for food crops, and harbours 12 types of tropical forest ecosystems. With only about 0.36 per cent of the world's land surface, Thailand has between 2 and 10 per cent of the world's vertebrate animals and higher plant species, includ-ing 10 per cent of all species of birds, nearly 5 per cent of monocotyledonous plants and almost 4 per cent of di-cotyledonous plants.

The area which is present-day Thailand has been culti-vated continuously by humans for at least 5,700 years. Ar-chaeological evidence has shown that the northeast region of the country is one of the world's oldest rice cultivation areas; farmers have been growing rice there for over 5,000 years. This region is still cultivated and many varieties of rice still grow there.

---

* Day-cha Siripatra and Witton Lianchamroon both work with the Thai NGO Technology for Rural and Ecological Enrichment (TREE), headquar-tered north of Bangkok. TREE has been the leading NGO among those involved in promoting sustainable agriculture which has developed a spe-cific and active programme on the conservation and enhancement of local genetic diversity for small-scale farming. Day-cha and Wittoon are among the main proponents of this work in Thailand.

But as in other developing countries, genetic resources in Thailand are being rapidly lost. Genetic erosion started decades ago and accelerated during the 1980s for many reasons. The most obvious causes are deforestation and reforestation. Thailand used to be covered with abundant natural forest but this is being cut down rapidly. In 1961, when Thailand launched its first national economic development plan, 53 per cent of the land was forested; ten years later, only 43 per cent of the land was forested. In 1990 it was estimated that only 15–17 per cent of the country's area was forest land.

The main causes of deforestation are logging by companies under legal concessions, illegal logging, expansion of field crop cultivation into the forests, and the construction of roads and dams. Besides this, the government's policy promoting the planting of fast-growing trees such as eucalyptus, by private companies in support of the wood and paper industries, has accelerated the rate of forest destruction; at the same time, coastal mangrove forests have been vastly damaged by the promotion of prawn-rearing industries.

The second major cause of genetic erosion in Thailand is the introduction of high-yielding varieties (HYVs) of crop plants on the expanding agricultural lands. Since 1961, the Thai government has continuously and extensively encouraged farmers to use HYVs instead of their traditional ones. The euphemistically named 'Local Varieties Exchange Programme' of the Ministry of Agriculture's Department of Agricultural Extension began in 1967, and has been a massive effort to replace farmer's indigenous landraces with a few genetically uniform HYVs. Agricultural officers were stationed throughout the countryside and farmers were invited to trade in their diverse and unique planting materials in exchange for new government seed. This way, no money was involved. In rice, many of the HYVs were based on materials developed at the International Rice Research Institute (IRRI). In maize, they were seeds of the TNCs, distributed through the government. The effect has been devastating, particularly in the irrigated areas. By 1980, HYVs covered half of the national crop lands. The use of local rice varieties in Thailand was further slashed from 45 per cent in 1981 to 24 per cent in 1986. What happened to the farmers' landraces collected by the government from the late 1960s until the early 1980s? As far as we know, they were used for animal feed. Conservation was not on the government's agenda.

Today, for the dry season (February to June) farmers now use HYVs for about 90 per cent of the rice area they cultivate. For the rainy season (July through October), on the other hand, farmers use recommended varieties on only half of their cultivated land, but for this they rely on fewer than five varieties. Another crop under the variety replacement scheme is the rubber tree. Farmers previously grew old rubber tree varieties from seed and in this way variation was promoted. Moreover they planted the trees in with fruit trees such as jack fruit, rambutan, durian and lanseh. The government's policy is to promote monocultures of new varieties in areas expanded to increase rubber production.

The Thai government has special programmes for plant breeding, seed selection, propagation and production for the economically important crops. These include rice, maize, sorghum, soybean, peanut, mung bean, cotton, sesame, castor, sugar cane, cassava and rubber. The 21 government plant propagation units all over the country can produce approximately 40,000 tonnes of improved seed per year. But foreign-owned companies also play a major part in promoting HYVs. The top five companies active in Thailand are all subsidiaries of major multinationals: Continental Grain, Ciba-Geigy, Dekalb, Pioneer and Cargill (by order of local turnover). They have total sales of over 50,000 tonnes of field crops every year. Thailand imports vegetable seed from foreign countries in the range of 440 tonnes per year; at the same time, the country exports about 300 tonnes of vegetable seed. All major exporting companies are also branches of overseas TNCs: Asgrow, Adam International, Sluis & Groot and Knov-Yoa Seed. In evidence of the success of this pro-HYV policy, the deputy-director general of the Thai government's Agriculture Extension Division was personally granted the International Seed Business Association's 'World Seed Award'.

Conservation: the approach of the formal sector

The government has both *in situ* and *ex situ* programmes for genetic resources conservation. The *in situ* work is mostly the responsibility of the Royal Forestry Department of the Ministry of Agriculture. The government's target is to conserve

15 per cent of the country's area as national forest in the form of parks, wildlife sanctuaries and wildlife hunting reserves, aside from botanical gardens and fruit tree and herb collection gardens. At present, the *in situ* genetic resources conservation area of Thailand covers some 150,000 square kilometres.

The *ex situ* collections are stored in two genebanks: the National Rice Germplasm Bank and the National Genebank of Thailand. The first was built in Pathumanthani with the support of the Japanese government in 1981. Funding included provisions for collecting rice to store in the genebank, but the programme lasted only five years. No governmental rice collecting was done before or after this period. There are about 20,000 varieties of rice under the care of this bank, over 80 per cent of which is local varieties of Thai rice. The rest is from Myanmar and other neighbouring countries, including some HYVs.

The second genebank was built in Bangkok with the support of the International Board for Plant Genetic Resources (IBPGR) in 1984. It has the capacity for at least 40,000 accessions, but at present holds only 2,600 varieties, mostly winged bean from Indonesia! IBPGR has supported the collection of about 14,000 accessions of different landraces in Thailand, but they aHe not in the IBPGR-sponsored genebank. We know that 3,600 samples were exported to the USA, more than the number that remain in the genebank now, but we have no idea what happened to the rest. Genebank officials have told local NGOs that the samples are the property of the germplasm collectors; those which were taken away cannot be traced and those which remain cannot be accessed without written permission.

NGOs: towards an integrated strategy

There are some 200 NGOs in Thailand, most of which deal with rural development in one way or another. Their work in genetic conservation is usually part of wider environmental, agricultural and rural development work. Many NGO activities take the form of campaigns against destructive development plans. The National Forest Protection Campaign resulted in the Thai government banning several logging concessions in 1989. In 1988, NGOs co-operated with students and other Thai people successfully to stop the building of the Nam Chon Dam which would have destroyed huge areas of forest for an electricity production scheme. In 1990, NGOs were holding up the construction of the Kang Krung Dam. There are, however, still six more plans for dam construction.

NGOs are working to solve the problem of landlessness among farmers by co-operating with other groups to get the government to take action. It is estimated that about 10 of the 35 million Thai farmers are landless and now live in the national forest, having converted about six million hectares of forest land to arable cultivation. If there is no solution to solve farmers' ownership problem, they will continue to encroach upon the national forest.

There are now 19 NGOs assembled as the Alternative Agriculture Group. Together, they are trying to investigate, develop and disseminate appropriate alternative agriculture technologies which are more suited to the Thai climate and local conditions than those of the Green Revolution. The alternatives involve integrated farming, with an emphasis on diversity of crop varieties and the use of local inputs.

TREE is part of the group. TREE has been promoting farming of fish integrated with rice production in the poor northeastern part of the country. The fish, which live and grow in the rice paddies, provide an important source of protein which complements the staple rice. The short-strawed HYVs are not suitable for this type of farming system since they do not grow in deeply flooded fields and the pesticides and fertilizers which they require kill all the fish. Because of this, TREE began collecting more suitable indigenous varieties in 1984 and distributing them free to farmers for them to test and use. So far, over 2,500 accessions of 30 crops have been collected. The programme has now expanded into sustainable agriculture, concerned with soils, biological pest control and conserving genetic resources. Conservation began only three years ago, based on the collections made from farmers' seed stocks throughout the country, including from among the hill tribe people and other areas hard to reach. We did not bother collecting seeds from markets or other obvious areas. From farmers we took just a little seed and multiplied it. TREE keeps one set. Duplicates of the collection are currently stored at the National Rice Germplasm Bank, until community seed banks can be established. At least 60 per cent of the rice varieties we have collected were not, up until now, represented in the government's collection. A third set is given for free to farmers for experimentation and testing.

The future priorities are to continue collecting, because the indigenous Thai varieties are disappearing rapidly; to multiply, evaluate, document and store the germplasm at the village level; and to get involved in grassroots breeding work. There is increasing co-operation with foreign NGOs. Over the two years 1988–9, NGOs working on the collection of local varieties developed contacts with similar groups in Indonesia, the Philippines and Laos. They exchanged ideas and experience about the collection and use of traditional seeds, and began to exchange local varieties.

In 1990, Thai NGOs hosted the first Asian community seed conservation and utilization training course, in co-operation with NGOs from the Philippines. Thirty participants from countries of south and southeast Asia took part in the three-week course. It is planned to repeat the event in 1992, but not necessarily in Thailand.

Conservation and use of plant genetic resources is a huge task which requires the co-operation of many groups, especially that of the indigenous farmers. Thai NGOs cannot make a big impact alone, but they can facilitate work with others. There are however, many obstacles to overcome, a major problem being to ensure continuity of the work. Genetic conservation and utilization necessarily takes a long time, but NGO projects are usually only for three to five years. Commitment for longer-term projects requires external financial support.

In the long run, the main task of genetic resource conservation should be undertaken by the farmers in co-operation with NGOs. The latter have an important role to play in linking up farmers and in promoting their concerns, such as the shortage of land. Community seed banks run by farmers should be set up to put the seed supply firmly under local control rather than that of government agencies or overseas companies.

5 Women and biological diversity: lessons from the Indian Himalaya

VANDANA SHIVA and IRENE DANKELMAN*

Women have traditionally played a silent yet central role in the management and sustainable use of biological resources and life support systems. Their relationship with their environment is holistic, multidimensional and productive. Western research and technology is undermining the control women have over these systems and breaking down the linkages that made evolution possible. Conservation of biological diversity will not be possible if women are marginalized from resource management and production.

Local knowledge about natural processes and resources has always been transmitted from generation to generation of women. Women's role in land use has been essential, concerning not only food production but water and fuel supply, and the provision of fodder, fibres, medicines and other natural products. Women were the original food producers all over the world and they continue to be central to food production systems in the Third World.

Yet only recently more attention has been paid to the hidden contribution of women to plant and animal domestication which occurred as human societies made the transition from gathering–hunting to agricultural and nomadic ways of life. The paradigm of man-the-hunter, based on assumptions of male dominance, competition, exploitation and aggression, is slowly giving way to alternative perceptions which recognize the contribution of woman-the-gatherer, and the interdependence of the sexes in making survival possible

* Vandana Shiva, physicist, philosopher and feminist, is one of India's most prominent movers in the struggle for the recognition, defence and development of the crucial role and place women have in managing biological diversity throughout the Third World. Vandana is director of the Research Foundation for Science, Technology and Natural Resource Policy in Dehra Dun. Irene Dankelman is a Dutch agronomist and teaches at the Agricultural University of Wageningen. For the past couple of years, she has been working with Vandana on issues relating to women and agriculture, with a particular focus on biodiversity.

through co-operation. In pre-agricultural societies, gathering contributed about 80 per cent of the food supply while hunting accounted for only 20 per cent.

Because food production requires a thorough knowledge of plant and animal growth, maturation and reproduction, women have had a crucial role in the domestication and cultivation of plants and animals. Food-gathering inventions attributable to women are the digging stick, the carrying sling, the sickle and other knives. A survey of advanced horticultural societies reveals that farming is the exclusive domain of women in one half of them, and shared with men on an equal footing in another quarter. Only in a little over one-fifth of these societies is agriculture the sole responsibility of men.[1]

It is obvious, especially where modern technology has been introduced, that the perceptions of local women of their natural environment and genetic resources are multidimensional, compared to those of men. As a consequence of existing power structures and the differences in gender roles and tasks, men often prefer commercial returns, as opposed to welfare returns to the family. Whereas a forest acts in the eyes of a women as a multifunctional system, men tend to focus on one or only a few outputs. The rationale for these differences can be found in the introduction of Western science and technology into the local agro-ecosystem, as it is based on a reductionist view and approach to the world. Also, the difference in interests between women and men leads to a differentiation of their environmental perceptions.

The hill and mountain economies of the Garhwal Himalaya

The Garhwal Himalaya region of India provides an example of the central role of women in agriculture and the management of biological resources. Women are the actual subsistence farmers of the hills.[2] In this hill and mountain economy, characterized by an integration of forest management, animal husbandry and agriculture, women play a predominant role. They work often more than 16 hours a day. The only agricultural work which is done by men is carried out with the help of bullocks. A study of one-hectare farm in the Indian Himalaya showed that in a year, a pair of bullocks works for 1,064 hours, a man for 1,212 and a woman for 3,485 hours. Another study showed that women in the hill agriculture of Himachal Pradesh do 37 per cent of the work in sowing, 59 per cent in interculture, 66 per cent in harvesting, 59 per cent in trenching and 69 per cent in tending the animals. This is apart from all the household chores, which include the collection of fuel and water.[3]

In the Hemwal Valley, for example, women do almost all of the farm work themselves in local paddy fields, including the selection of seeds of indigenous rice varieties. Women rice growers in central Libena use and recognize well over 100 varieties of rice. They know everything about the cultivation practices of each variety as well as other features, such as the ease with which the husk can be removed, the length of time required for cooking, and each variety's suitability to different ecological conditions.

Women's role in seed selection and vegetative propagation is crucial not only in agricultural production but also in the conservation and enhancement of genetic resources. In a sample participatory study with women hill farmers in Dehra Dun, we were provided with no less than 145 species of forest plants which women know and use. The hill and mountain economy is one in which forest, crops and livestock management are closely interlinked. Women's work and knowledge is particularly relevant to these linkages, through which ecological stability and sustainability is maintained. Women's labour, through the collection of fodder, fuel and minor forest products, is crucial in enabling the resource flows necessary to keep the economy running in a sustainable way.

It appears that women maintain a high degree of autonomy in the hill and mountain areas. This is evident if you look at some of the more important factors which determine whether or not women can control their own lives. First, in these traditional agro-ecosystems, women have considerable access to and control over the means of production, that is, the forests, land and land use, animals and other biological resources. Through systems by which knowledge is passed on from mother to daughter, they also have access to and control over training and education. However, while women doubtless have considerable control over their own labour, in reality much of it reflects pure necessity; men will also exercise some control over women's time. Second, women do have some control over forms of organization amongst themselves, resulting from the amount of time they spend together working in groups. The Chipko movement in the Himalaya provides a striking example of collective effort to preserve the forest ecosystem. Third, with regard to control over women's sexuality and fertility, it might be deduced from the stable populations of these areas that women practise birth control measures. On the other hand, pregnancy and birth are not extraordinary states and women in their third trimester of pregnancy will still be found working in the field. Finally, women's sense of dignity and self-respect and their right to self-determination might be indicated from cultural expressions in their songs and dances and their resistance to modernization and commercialization processes. What is also striking is the fact that women are usually very much aware of the conflicts between their interests and those of their husbands in the management of natural resources.

The displacement of women in biodiversity management

Research in Garhwal reveals that the shift from subsistence to commercial agriculture, through the introduction of cash crops and the market economy, has led to a reduction in women's sphere of influence and an increasing dependence of women on men for extension services, purchase of seeds and handling of tools and money. The disappearance of indigenous forests has meant that women have to walk further to collect forest products; and whereas local women used to be able to list 145 species of trees and their uses, the new forestry experts, in contrast, could name only 25, which highlights the differences in knowledge of genetic resources between local inhabitants and external experts. Women's crucial role in agriculture is gradually diminished by the introduction of new agrotechnology and crop varieties, which are aimed at male farmers. The woman's role becomes more and more that of a labourer as she loses her control over production and access to resources.

The replacement of local varieties with new, introduced high-yielding ones (HYVs) leads to resource scarcity in the farming system. The shift, for example, from local pulses to introduced soybean implies a shift from domestic to industrial food processing, displacing women from their local resources. Current agricultural research concentrates heavily on increasing the yield of only certain parts of the crop, often those which can be commercially marketed. For example, traditional potato and mustard varieties provide

47

fresh leaf vegetables in the mountain diets. The HYVs of these crops do not.

In the Herwal valley, where the women used to grow many indigenous varieties of rice, the HYVs are completely directed at men and at commercial interests. Dwarf varieties which are promoted through the Green Revolution reduce the straw available for fodder and fertilizer, which are essential components of women's sustainable agricultural systems. A reduction in straw leads to a reduction in organic matter, thus contributing to declining soil fertility.

Weeding is predominantly women's work. The increased fertilizer use that is intrinsically required by HYVs has stimulated weed growth dramatically, further increasing women's work burden. The off-season vegetable farming for export, presently one of the most popular development strategies for hill agriculture, has had similar effects. The replacement of millet and other coarse grains by vegetables for export not only reduces local food availability but lowers the production of fodder.

Dairy development schemes aimed at the marketing of milk have led to a monopolization by rich landowners of fodder resources of the village commons and the denial of access to poorer women to collect fodder. As a Haryan woman put it, 'Now I have to steal the grass for my buffalo and when the landlord catches me, he beats me.' More and more evidence shows that the women are unable to manage the cross-bred animals, as their feed and other requirements are quite different from that of the indigenous cattle. The concentrate feeds required by the new cattle change the composition of cow dung, making it unsuitable for women's use in managing soil structure.

Reversing the trend

The introduction of new agrotechnologies within the current industrial–commercial market systems results in resource fragmentation, undermining the position of women. The flows of a biomass resources, that is, plant material for food, fodder and fuel, as well as animal wastes, traditionally maintained by women are disturbed and the different linkages between the agriculture, forests and livestock sectors of the system break down. Instead, inputs and outputs become completely dependent on external markets.

This process has a number of adverse effects on women and their management of natural resources:

○ The replacement of local varieties and biological diversity leads to the loss of sources of food, fuel, fodder and minor forest products essential to meet the needs of women and their families. The increased vulnerability of the system makes women's position more uncertain.
○ Women lose control over management of natural resources, and they also lose their control over labour as a result of changing structures and the increases in their work burdens.
○ The deskilling and de-intellectualizing of women, through the ignorance of their contribution to management, knowledge and experience of the agro-ecosystem, results in a loss of women's knowledge and intellectual integrity with regard to forestry, agriculture, plant genetic resources and animal husbandry. Women also lose their status and decision-making power in the social system, breaking down their sense of dignity, self-respect and self determination.

We expect that biotechnology, in the way it is now being developed, will not only reinforce these trends but also deepen them. Not only will sustainable resource flows be broken down, but also the natural evolutionary and local breeding mechanisms will be undermined by the new technologies. This will worsen even further women's autonomy and the life-support systems they and their families depend upon. The ultimate ecological and cultural impact of these new technologies will be the annihilation of diversity and sustainability in nature and, as a direct consequence, of basic human needs and rights.

To reverse this trend:

○ There is a great need for baseline studies on women's knowledge, experience, roles and position in managing the agro-ecosystems all over the world. These studies should aim at improving women's access to and control over these resources and systems.
○ The development and introduction of new technologies should be based on the needs, participation and position improvement of local women and their environment. For this purpose gender impact assessments must be carried

out to determine whether or not the technologies should be introduced further.

○ In conserving natural resources, the access to and control over these resources by local women should be guaranteed and improved.

○ Development projects which do not guarantee or improve women's autonomy and access to and control over resources should be abandoned in favour of those which improve these factors.

The successful management of biological resources is dependent on woman's control over the environment and her production systems. Unless the role of women is respected and reinforced, conservation of genetic diversity will not succeed.

On-farm selection allows for the production of a wide range of locally adapted varieties.

One of the many traditional rice varieties. Southeast Asia is one of the centres of diversity for rice; Indonesia alone has more than 13,000 indigenous varieties. Farmers' organizations are playing an increasingly important role in conserving this genetic heritage.

A rice farmer in Indonesia. Over 100 million people live on Java island and most are dependent on rice as a staple food. Diversity of varieties is therefore especially important to their security.

Small grain cereals like sorghum are vital to Zimbabwe's food security. Besides being drought tolerant, their seeds remain viable for several seasons of storage and they require lower inputs to cultivate. All these factors contribute to increased self-reliance for small-scale farmers.

6 Promoting traditional trees and food plants in Kenya

KIHIKA KIAMBI and MONICA OPOLE*

Genetic resources of local crops and trees play an important role in subsistence farming in Kenya. However, the colonial legacy continues to under-rate and undermine these resources. In a broad attempt to reverse these trends, Kenya Energy and Environment Organizations (KENGO) has been promoting the conservation and use of traditional trees and food crops in Kenya by supporting the practical activities of its member groups, through raising public awareness on the value of indigenous knowledge about traditional plants, and through joint research activities with national institutions.

With their country's population close to 25 million and with an annual increase of 4 per cent, Kenyans today are increasingly aware of the problems they face in order to feed themselves, to produce sufficient fuelwood for domestic needs, and to sustain biological diversity for the provision of fodder, fruits, dyes, tannins, gums, resins, and medicines. Only 17–20 per cent of the country's total land area is suitable for agricultural production and it is from this land that about 90 per cent of the population depends for a living.

It has been estimated that there are about 8,000–9,000 species of plants in Kenya. Two thousand of these are trees and shrubs, of which 5 per cent are considered endangered while about 8 per cent are rare. Up to about one fifth of all the herbaceous plant species may be endangered. Policies

* Dionysious Kihika Kiambi now works at the International Board for Plant Genetic Resources' (IBPGR) regional office in Nairobi. Until recently he was Natural Resources Programme manager at Kenya Energy and Environment Organization (KENGO). Trained in conservation of plant genetic resources, he has many years of experience of promoting community projects and organizing workshops and training programmes. Monica Opole manages KENGO's Indigenous Food Plants Project. She has worked in a variety of community-based schemes concerning energy conservation through the use of fuel-efficient stoves as well as conservation of biological resources.

and programmes must be developed for the conservation of biodiversity and genetic resources if medical, agricultural and technological advances are to be made. The magnitude of the task is great; the continued stability of the country's environment and habitat depends largely on these resources. This is now being slowly realized by policy makers, scientists and environmentalists.

At the local level, rural communities are faced with serious depletion of biological diversity upon which they rely so much. Conservation efforts have been seriously constrained by lack of technical, moral and financial support. Where rural communities are sensitized, and awareness of the importance of biodiversity conservation is high, the infrastructure to initiate and maintain conservation projects is often missing. Many externally led programmes often fail both to involve the communities in planning and to identify them as the intended beneficiaries of the initiatives; even more often, such programmes have institutionalized academic objectives which over-ride the communities' conservation needs and priorities. Many efforts fail to understand that these communities are the custodians of biodiversity and that they know its value and potential. It is a prerequisite for successful conservation policies that communities be involved in all decisions which have a bearing on biological resources, from project formulation to planning and implementation.

Kenya's germplasm heritage

East Africa is geographically and ecologically diverse with ecosystems ranging from deserts to tropical rainforests. The lowland areas are predominantly arid, within which pockets of humid environments have formed from highlands, wetlands and the Rift Valley. Ecologically, this has created a strong diversity of habitats. One area with a high species diversity is Kakamega Forest in Western Kenya, the easternmost relict of the Guineo-Congolean tropical rainforests; others include the forests of the Mau escarpment, Mount Kenya and Aberdare, and the coastal forests. Of the total land area of 570,000 square kilometres, only about 4 per cent is under forest. The remaining indigenous forests might be considered for *in situ* conservation, although current pressures will make this objective hard to achieve.

The Abyssinian centre of diversity, in its broad sense,

stretches to cover much of the country, and many of our traditional crops could be considered to belong to this Vavilov centre. This is exemplified by the wide distribution of many wild relatives of cultivated plants, including coffee, sorghum, millet, *Vigna*, sesame, lablab (hyacinth bean), and others.

Pre-colonial Kenya was characterized by a rich biological diversity found in the vast indigenous forests which sprawled the country and was relatively undisturbed due to low population densities. The diversity of primitive cultivars, landraces and wild species gave rise to thousands of plants being used as sources of local food. These food plants, which became a part of folk culture, included wild fruits, annuals and perennials, potherbs, roots and tubers, legumes, vegetables, aquatic weeds and partially domesticated crops of all types. The list of edible plants and local crops used by all the ethnic groups in Kenya probably goes into the hundreds, although no comprehensive list has been compiled for the whole country. All these crops are highly adapted to their environments and have developed disease resistance through co-evolution with their pests and pathogens. They require minimal inputs of labour or management. It has been verified that some of them are often superior in taste and/or nutritional quality to the introduced varieties.

The country's arid and semi-arid lands have much to offer in terms of plant resources, with possibilities of wider cultivation and commercial exploitation. The commercial use of gum arabica from *Acacia senegal* and collection of myrrh incense or resins from *Commiphora* spp. could contribute greatly to the national economy. The potential is some way from realization, and the marketing of these commodities is left largely unorganized. Properly used, this genetic resource base could lessen Kenya's dependence on food aid and make its mark on the country's economy through increased exports.

The colonial legacy

The status of the country's biological diversity and genetic resources changed dramatically through colonialism. The introduction of exotic forest species brought on the clearing of massive areas of indigenous forests to grow uniform monocultures of forest plantations, mainly to produce timber for

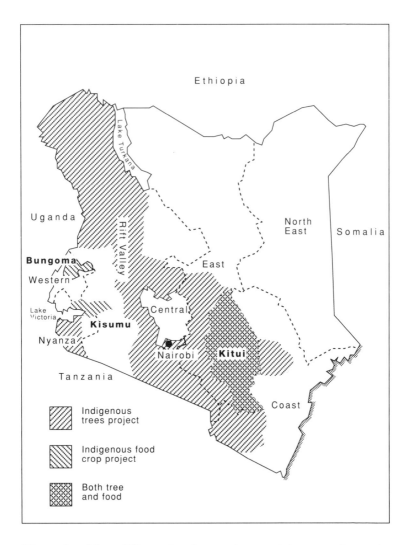

Figure 3. *Map of Kenya showing provinces and the areas of operation of KENGO projects. The Indigenous Trees Project is operated in a large part of the country, including the arid areas of the north-west; the semi-arid areas of the Rift Valley, Eastern and Coastal provinces and the medium production lands of South Nyanza. The Indigenous Food Crops Project is focused on two regions: the relatively high production areas of Western Kenya (Bungoma and Kisumu Districts) and the semi-arid Kitui District.*

export to the colonial power. These few fast-growing species of such genera as pine, eucalyptus and cypress have a uniform and narrow genetic base. This practice, now well entrenched, for a long time led to near total neglect of conservation and research on local species; more recently, the problem has been compounded by expanding populations which continue to open up indigenous forests for cash-crop and subsistence agriculture.

The breakdown and fragmentation of natural habitats, with massive loss of biodiversity and wild relatives of cultivated crops, are consequences of these combined factors. As this loss occurred before any inventory was done we do not know what we have lost, but we do know that the potential of these resources to address current agricultural, technological or medical problems will never be realized. The continuing over-exploitation of some other species of economic importance poses a threat to their existence and to their genetic diversity, for example African ebony, which the handicraft trade has exploited to near extinction due to demand from the tourist industry, and Camphor wood and African velvet.

A further serious blow to genetic resources has been the introduction of new crops which undermine traditional diets, themselves already threatened by the erosion of ethnic cultures and traditions. The colonialists' condemnation of traditional food crops, which were for a long time seen as inferior, primitive or marginal, led to their abandonment, particularly by so-called educated communities. The greatest loss of Kenyan genetic resources may, however, be attributed to the impact of the Green Revolution, which has seemingly increased food production with its introduction of new, improved or hybrid cultivars in food and cash crops. The Kenya National Food Policy of 1984 stated clearly that the objective of food crops research will be to continue the search for more productive varieties, with the emphasis of breeding programmes being on continuous yield increases. Though absolute food yields may have risen initially, when hybrid and other 'miracle' seeds were used by farmers their genetic uniformity made them highly vulnerable to pests and diseases. In addition, they require high levels of costly chemical inputs such as fertilizers and pesticides, and farmers have to purchase seeds every season.

There has been a heavy reliance on imported germplasm in the country's plant-breeding programmes and only token utilization of the local varieties, which may confer such important characteristics as environmental adaptability and disease resistance. Landraces, which have taken generations to develop and are well adapted to local conditions and environmental stresses, have been or are being rapidly replaced or wiped out by 'improved' cultivars. The pros and cons of increased exports through a cash-crop economy *vis-à-vis* the potential accrued benefit of conservation of genetic resources and its contribution to food production call for a serious evaluation, particularly at this time when real prices of exports are falling in international markets.

The country is faced with severe erosion of valuable genes nurtured and carried over from generation to generation in different seed varieties and sustained as part of peoples' cultural heritage. Though widely and generally neglected by commercial sectors, unique food crops are still used in mainly rural and peasant communities, where women know the nutritional needs of their families and the nutritive and medicinal qualities of the crops.

KENGO's approach

KENGO is a coalition of women's groups, farmers' organizations and other local NGOs involved in environmental conservation, wood-energy use and community development. It was founded in 1981 following the UN Conference on New and Renewable Energy held in Nairobi, and its secretariat provides technical and material support to member NGOs. For seven years now, KENGO's National Resources Programme, through the Seeds and Genetic Resources Project, has been promoting the conservation and utilization of indigenous plants for their economic usefulness as food and sources of several other rural requirements such as fibres, dyes, fuelwood, fodder and medicines.

The programme dates back to 1982 when KENGO realized that the genetic diversity of indigenous plants was threatened with depletion due to the introduction of exotic species. Its initial objective was to sensitize both the decision makers and the general public to the need to conserve these vital resources and to promote their sustainable use at the community level. An ethnobotanical data collection of indigenous trees in arid and semi-arid lands was launched. Eight districts have so far been covered, resulting in the collection of 120 specimens of economically important indigenous trees. Data were collected through interviews with elderly people, who provided a wealth of information on medicinal, fuelwood, agroforestry, fodder, food and sociocultural uses of these trees. These have now been compiled and will be published soon in the form of a *Resource Book of Indigenous Trees of the Arid and Semi-Arid Areas of Kenya*.

The promotional and publicity campaigns on conservatives of indigenous plants were well received at both popular and official levels and led to an explosion of interest and requests for seed. People wanted more information on the uses and potential uses of indigenous plants, which species should be used where, how to get hold of seed, how to handle it, and so on. KENGO found that the lack of availability of seed and of the technical know-how on propagation (vegetative or seed) of indigenous plants were major constraints to conservation efforts. The programme therefore initiated the Seeds and Genetic Resources Project with the objectives to identify *in situ* seed resources, to process and distribute indigenous trees and food plant seeds, to carry out simple and repeatable propagation techniques, and to develop curriculum and educational materials for training in seed collection and handling. A vital component of the project is to raise awareness and promote institutional linkages in all aspects of seeds and genetic resources work. This is done through exhibits, seminars, workshops, publications and travelling expeditions. One expedition on threatened habitats in Kenya led to a controversial debate on whether or not to drain an important wetland area, the Yala swamp.

An early product of the project was the publication of *A Pocket Directory of Trees and Seeds in Kenya*, which comprises of short profiles of common trees in Kenya and their seed sources. Other publications include a status report of *Seeds and Genetic Resources in Kenya*, a report of proceedings of *National Expedition on Genetic Resources and Habitats* and an easy-to-read booklet on *How to collect, handle and store seeds* targeted at community-based afforestation programmes. Publications are distributed through KENGO's national membership structure, during community, local and national workshops, and as part of the extension packages used by the KENGO field extension programme which provides technical and material assistance to grassroots organizations carrying out afforestation and conservation projects.

The project continues to procure and distribute seeds, and to organize specialized and non-specialized training courses in seed collection and handling. So far, about 700kg of indigenous plants seeds have been obtained and distributed to 400 destinations including schools, local and foreign NGOs, government ministries, individual farmers and research institutions. Forty seed collectors have been trained in theoretical and practical aspects of the job. They now form the backbone of KENGO's seed collection and distribution network.

An important turning point in the project was the incorporation of a pilot research and conservation component. The research and *ex situ* conservation of economically important indigenous trees is a joint undertaking between KENGO and the Jomo Kenyatta University College of Agriculture, which donated 15 acres of land for the project activities. As part of the joint work, seed viability tests, presowing treatments and propagation trials have been conducted on 35 species. Field genebanks have been set up for the *ex situ* conservation of economically important indigenous forest and fruit trees. In all, 2,900 specimens of 86 species have been conserved in the project site. KENGO and the university have undertaken joint research on nursery management and the monitoring of tree growth performances to identify the conditions for faster growth.

In the course of its conservation efforts, KENGO realized the potential of indigenous plants to diversity the food base and provide better nutrition at a community level. This gave rise to the Indigenous Fruits and Vegetables Development Project, which currently encompasses all traditional food crops. It aims to encourage the conservation of indigenous fruits and vegetables through increased use at the community level.

Several botanical surveys to collect samples of fruits and vegetables have been conducted, resulting in a collection of 66 fruit samples and 35 vegetable samples from areas where diversity of these food plants is still high, mainly in Eastern and Western Kenya. The fruits and vegetables are assessed for nutritional quality through collaboration with the Kenya Industrial Research Institute and the Crop Science and Food Science and Technology Department of Nairobi University. Very encouraging results have been achieved. Some indigenous fruits and vegetables such as *Adansonia digitata* (baobab) and *Gynandropsis gynandra* have proved to contain higher nutritional qualities than common introduced fruit and vegetable species such as kale and cabbage. Agronomic trials and seed bulking of a few priority indigenous vegetables have begun, with the objective of distributing the seeds to farmers for wider-scale trials.

Sample products have already been developed from several indigenous fruits and vegetables. Fruits can be used to make juices, jams, chutneys and food flavours; vegetables can be dried, powdered or precooked to form infant foods. The objective is to interest food industries to incorporate these samples in their finished products. Plans are under way to carry out feasibility studies for community-based processing units. Combined with demand from industries, this initiative may go a long way in encouraging farmers to grow more indigenous foodstuffs as marketing channels will be available, enabling the farmer to get some much-needed income as an incentive for conservation.

The initiatives supported by KENGO through its Natural Resources Programme include both those of individual farmers and those of grassroots NGOs. One such initiative has been made by Mrs Mwongela Muimi of Kitui district in Eastern Kenya. On a 18-hectare farm, she has conserved more than 15 different economically important species. From afar, the steep slopes of the hill appear to be nothing but dense thicket. At closer proximity the bush reveals the most mouth watering native fruits: *matote, ngala, ngomoa,* and *tamarind.* These types of fruits are becoming more and more difficult to acquire in the district due to clearing of indigenous vegetation for agricultural use and other purposes.

Mrs Muimi claims that the indigenous fruits do not need any special management and that they are not easily attacked by diseases. Their diversity allows her family to benefit throughout the year as the fruits ripen at different times. KENGO has taken samples from her farm for nutritional analysis and the results have shown that some, such as tamarind, have exceptionally high nutritional quality. This information encourages and supports her in her efforts to conserve the indigenous fruits instead of clearing the bushes to plant less-adapted and more disease-prone exotic fruit species.

The programme supports not only individual farmers but

also community-based grassroots NGOs, for example the Olembo women's group which farms near the shores of Lake Victoria. The group is re-introducing traditional trees, fruits and vegetables into its farming systems and taking advantage of the many benefits which these local plants provide. The Ober tree (*Albizia coriaria*), for example, provides wood for timber and fuel, leaves for covering ripening bananas and for the children to play with, and the bark can be cooked up to make a medicine which is good for children's ailments. Vegetables have multiple uses too. 'Spider Weed' (*Gynandropsis gynandra*), or 'Dek' in the local Luo language, makes a nutritive vegetable meal used widely for treating protein and vitamin deficiencies; extracts are used to relieve aching eyes. Other traditional vegetables such as 'Dodo' *(Amaranthus)*, 'Atipe' *(Asystecia schimperi)*, and 'Mitoo' *(Corchorus olitorius)*, are used to add flavour and improve the nutritive value of staple foods like *ugali*, the typical maize meal.

Nyambera, another woman's group, lies in a sugar-belt located in western Kenya. Comprised of 40 members, the group's conservation initiatives stemmed from the grassroots after people realized that their natural resources were seriously depleted and it was only with difficulty that they could obtain the plants they needed as sources of firewood, fodder, medicines, dyes and tannins. These plants are badly depleted due to encroachment of indigenous forests for sugarcane production and other socio-economic infrastructures. In 1986 the group registered as a member of KENGO, which provided indigenous tree seeds and other multipurpose species for seedling production in the group nursery. Over the years, KENGO has also provided material assistance such as wheelbarrows, watering cans and fencing wire.

The indigenous plant seedlings produced are shared among the members and grown along the sugarcane plantations. These plants include fruit, fuelwood, fodder and medicinal species. The group produces 15,000–20,000 seedlings annually and a survival rate of 60 per cent is normally recorded. Some members have been trained by KENGO on several aspects of environmental conservation, including seed collection and handling, afforestation and wood-energy conservation.

The group's conservation activities have now been recognized by the surrounding community. The demand for seedlings has increased and the group is now selling them at nominal prices for income generation, an activity which has become self-sustainable. The group collects its own seeds locally, produces seedlings and sells them to the immediate community. Depending on the demand it collects seeds of trees it thinks are needed most by the community. KENGO no longer provides material assistance to the group but continues to provide technical advice on conservation matters.

Lessons from KENGO's experience

The work of KENGO and its member groups has helped to restore confidence in indigenous knowledge and the value of traditional trees and food crops. Their experience has shown that the popular belief that indigenous trees are slow growing is not entirely true. With proper management some local species can grow as fast as some popular exotic species; nor are indigenous trees difficult to propagate. Most of them can be regenerated through seed. Nutritional analyses have also shown that indigenous fruits and vegetables are not inferior in either nutritional or agronomic quality compared with introduced species. However, agricultural trials and genetic improvement are necessary in order to increase fruit and vegetable yields.

Further to all this, it has been clearly demonstrated that farm communities can be charged with conservation responsibilities especially if conservation objectives can be harmonized with short-term needs of the farmer. Creation of awareness is an important tool for enhancement of conservation objectives.

There are, however, major constraints to face. The erosion of cultural and traditional values has had a negative impact on the conservation and continued utilization of indigenous plants. These food plants have long been associated with poverty and backwardness, which makes their reintroduction difficult, unless conservation efforts are closely linked with public education and awareness campaigns. Conflicting messages from government, development agencies and NGO extension workers on emphasis and priorities for both conservation and farm productivity often confuse farmers and can exacerbate the problem.

For example, while the Ministry of Environment and Natural Resources advises farmers to plant trees in agroforestry schemes to promote self-sufficiency in fodder and fuelwood, the Ministry of Agriculture discourages tree planting on farmland claiming that it introduces new crop pests. Similarly, the Ministry of Environment and Natural Resources conflicts with KENGO on the relative value of indigenous and exotic species, the agriculture people stressing the high yields of exotics. There are also some differences between NGOs. For example the Greenbelt Movement encourages tree planting by giving money to farmers for every tree planted. KENGO believes that this approach has shortcomings since, after receiving the money, the farmers may no longer attach any importance to the tree. Instead, KENGO emphasizes the raising of awareness of the value of the trees, including their long-term and indirect benefits. Attempts to resolve these conflicts are now being made through increased technical collaboration and dialogue facilitated by the District Development Committee, made up of representatives from the major development agencies in each district as well as ministry officials.

The question of economic returns resurfaces frequently at the community level. Farmers will tend to give priority to crops which will give them good returns in terms of their family's daily needs. Marketing channels for most indigenous food plants have not yet been established, though a few popular ones are now emerging in local and urban markets.

Although conservation is something that has always been a concern to legal authorities, the current legal framework on natural resources is underdeveloped, and this presents additional constraints for community-level projects. Much legislation is based on the early colonial laws which laid emphasis on habitat protection *per se* to the total exclusion of *ex situ* conservation and of conservation through utilization. Although modifications to the law have been made, they remain inadequate. A major development has been in the area of seed legislation and management of plant varieties, which saw the establishment of the Seeds and Plant Varieties Act in 1972. The act formed a legal and institutional framework for the regulation of seed trade and plant breeding. Among other things, it was supposed to confer power to regulate transaction in seeds, establish an index of names of varieties and grant proprietary rights to breeders. Worth noting is the fact that there is no regulation on collection and export of species; likewise no legal machinery exists to control the introduction of new species and hybrid seeds.

Although there are several legal provisions which are supposed to provide direction and control of genetic resources in the country, their introduction has been fragmentary. There is no legal framework for the control, co-ordination or conservation of genetic resources *ex situ*, and although there are genebank facilities and activities, their operations take place in a legal vacuum.

The need for a broader approach

It is important to formulate and develop a national policy on the conservation and management of plant genetic resources since the current fragments of policy are truncated, conflicting and not legally binding. In particular there is a need to build an enabling form of legislation which will encompass all aspects of research, conservation, utilization, management, and local and international trade in genetic resources and technological innovations which might emerge from the new biotechnologies. At the same time, the need to raise awareness on the importance of national germplasm conservation remains. Progress has been made among scientists, policy makers and rural communities, but much remains to be done.

The scope of genetic resources activities in Kenya is great and points to scientific challenges to address the many development problems which could be tackled effectively by rational and sustainable use of plant genetic resources in the country. Agricultural research attempts to address the question of food security by fostering production for self-sufficiency. There is a need to boost the development and use of novel or 'poor man's' crops and the use of local landraces and primitive cultivars in plant-breeding programmes; these may go a long way towards the achievement of the National Food Policy goals. A national bio-database with efficient data acquisition, storage and retrieval systems and facilities is an important consideration. It should be introduced together with a national biological survey and inventories in the country's major centres of diversity. The data may become a management tool for facilitating further the conservation, development and rational use of plant genetic resources. Conservation of genetic resources must essentially employ diverse strategies in order to overcome the shortcomings of any one method. The current genebank approach is not likely to focus on the poor peoples' crops as they are not considered of national importance and may be uneconomical to store.

Conservation efforts stemming from the community level have the goal of conserving the genetic resources base through the continued use of the communities' priority crops. Their efforts are not always recognized or rewarded; though very important to particular communities, these genetic resources are not likely to have immediate economic significance at either the national or international levels and are far removed from commercial forces. While their survival largely depends on community conservation initiatives, this could be aided and encouraged by a coherent national policy as outlined above.

The involvement of local communities in conservation of biodiversity and genetic resources may result in greater effectiveness, because it encourages local people's sense of responsibility in resource management. Such involvement will depend on the value of the material and its contribution to immediate local needs, such as food, fodder and medicines. It is the rural communities which know which plants need to be conserved as they are the first to feel the impact of loss when these plants become rare. They can often identify threatened plants which may easily escape the eyes of the scientists. They have depository information on the range of plants available in their immediate environment. After all, they are the custodians of these vital resources.

Women constitute a large proportion of farmers in Zimbabwe. Here, one of ENDA's farmers' groups is discussing their programme and planning to hold a field day. Farmers' groups decide on the types of crops to be grown and the selection of farmers to carry out the studies.

A farmer inspecting the sorghum varieties during a field day. Field days are held at least once a year and they provide important feedback to the project from a large number of local farmers.

Women farmers at a landrace conservation and enhancement farm at Ataye, Southeast Shewa, Ethiopia, displaying their selections of sorghum. Farmers select for improved characteristics such as pest and disease resistance, earliness and nutritional and cooking qualities.

Trainees at a regional workshop organized by the Plant Genetic Resources Centre observing local farmers select sorghum landraces at their conservation farms at Ataye, Shewa.

7 Zimbabwean farmers as the starting point

ANDREW MUSHITA*

Genetic resources are a life-or-death matter in Zimbabwe, where drought can easily undermine a farmer's harvest. Against the push for hybrid maize, ENDA has been promoting well-adapted small grain cereals as the basis for food security in the region. But food security won't be achieved unless farmers control their resources, research capacities, storage and production systems. The Indigenous Seeds Project is working to make folkseed, and the people who developed them, the cornerstone of sustainable development.

Zimbabwe lies south of the equator within the Tropic of Capricorn, covering a total area of 400,000 square kilometres. The altitude varies from a maximum of over 2,500 metres above sea level in the Eastern Highlands, where tea and coffee plantations are concentrated on the best land, to 150 metres in the southeastern corner of the country. Between these lies the fertile central plateau with an average elevation of around 1,400 metres. Most of the large towns and industrial centres in Zimbabwe are situated along the plateau, which generally separates the drier southern and western parts of the country from the wetter northern and eastern parts. The major area of high agricultural potential is located on the central plateau around Harare. The summer rainfall of 750–1,000 millimetres tends to be reliable and supports maize, the country's staple food crop, as well as tobacco, cotton, wheat, other grain crops and intensive livestock production. In the Midlands region to the south,

* Andrew Mushita is an agronomist working with Environment and Development Action (ENDA-Zimbabwe), an NGO active in promoting sustainable agriculture and food security among small farmers. He has been centrally involved in the work of the Zimbabwe Seeds Action Network and the Indigenous Seeds Project. In the past years Andrew has helped ENDA's genetic resources activities provide a platform for strengthening national dialogue on genetic resources and biotechnology, and for broadening concerns for genetic diversity as a cornerstone to food security in the whole Southern Africa Development Coordination Conference (SADCC) region.

rainfall is lower, more intense and more variable. Cropping is risky, particularly for maize, which requires large quantities of moisture at specific periods of time for plant development. Recent studies by the World Bank revealed that Zim-

Figure 4. *Map of Zimbabwe showing the main natural regions. The pilot areas of the Indigenous Seeds Project are located in the arid and semi-arid areas, in the periphery of the country, corresponding to the 'Communal Lands' where most subsistence food production takes place. Commercial farming takes place mostly in the better lands of the fertile central plain, and the Eastern Highlands.*

babwe, an agricultural 'success story', had one of the highest rates of malnutrition among children below ten years. This may mean that people are cultivating cash crops at the expense of food crops, and are not buying enough food for their families. In 1987 some Z$84 million was spent in food distribution and public work projects for the estimated 1.4 million people affected by the drought. This bleak situation highlights the need to look deeper into the lack of food security at the grassroots level and the reasons behind it.

Traditional small grains for food security

To assure food security, a farming system must meet the minimum nutritional requirements of a household over at least a nine-month period. Small grains (sorghum and millets), particularly local varieties, are more likely to meet such needs than high-yielding maize hybrids; they are more drought tolerant, their seeds store much longer, and they can be relied upon to germinate even after several seasons of storage. Therefore farmers can depend on themselves rather than on the market for seed. As a risk-aversion measure, cultivation of small grains should be encouraged.

Small grains require fewer capital inputs than hybrid varieties. Intercropping, as opposed to monoculture, can reduce farmer's vulnerability to drought. Traditional varieties also contain genetic diversity, which is invaluable to breeders in search of genes for disease control and pest resistance, and other traits. Palatability is a determining factor in the use of traditional grains. Farmers have developed experience and knowledge over the years on the use of different crop cultivars for preparation of staple foods such as *sadza*. The grain quality has to meet certain criteria, such as sweet taste and good texture, and it should not stick in the hands or crack after being cooked. Some of the hybrids which do not meet one or more of these criteria are more likely to be cultivated as cash crops rather than for home consumption. Storage quality is also important. Some, indeed many, of the hybrids do not store well or require chemical treatment at least twice every season. Traditional small grains, on the other hand, store for up to five seasons. Greater use of traditional varieties should also allow reduced dependence on pesticides, important to small farmers since the costs of insecticides are increasing rapidly.

The Government of Zimbabwe, through the Ministry of Lands Agriculture and Rural Resettlement, has recently addressed the issue of food crops by forming a Sorghum and Millets Working Group. The objectives of this group, on which NGOs like ENDA sit, is to plan the use of small grains resources in Zimbabwe. Increased production and consumption of small grains is considered a priority. The Research Council of Zimbabwe has also recognized the value of traditional varieties (folkseed). The past three years of drought have demonstrated the value of sorghum and millet in afflicted areas. Unlike maize, sorghum and millet are relatively drought tolerant and can be grown successfully in marginal areas, while recent attempts by communal farmers to grow maize in these regions have proved disastrous during the drought years. The government's view is now becoming policy and farmers are encouraged to grow more small grains.

The Indigenous Seeds Project

Within this framework, the Indigenous Seeds Project is geared to strengthening farmer-based seed supply for indigenous food crops, particularly the small grains, in drought-prone areas of the country. The project is co-ordinated by ENDA-Zimbabwe and other member groups of the Zimbabwe Seeds Action Network (ZSAN). It was prompted by the need to develop appropriate varieties and recommendations for increasing the production of indigenous small grains in communal farming systems. Recognizing the important role played by communal farmers in the decision-making processes, the scheme is based on a participatory approach involving farmers' groups. These groups make the key decisions, including the type of crops to be grown in each area and the selection of farmers to carry out the studies. The project is not only directed at on-site research of local farming systems but also seeks to maximize the local control of such resources by the people themselves. It focuses on six separate but related components:

○ exploration and collection of indigenous crops;
○ seed cleaning, documentation and in-field characterization;
○ seed conservation, both at centralized and local levels;
○ varietal improvement and seed multiplication;

72

○ in-field agronomy trials;
○ communication and networking.

The five pilot project areas are located in the semi-arid and arid regions which consist of the southwestern third of the country and a smaller area in the northeast. With less than 650mm of rainfall annually, only drought-tolerant crops can be grown successfully and livestock production is the only sound basis of the farming system. However, these regions are vital for the food security of about three million people, over a third of the country's population. Over half of the population lives in communal areas, and almost three-quarters of these lie in the arid and semi-arid regions.

Since farmers have been and continue to be the backbone of the project, they are responsible for electing their own local seed committees. Each village selects two of its own members who, together with representatives from other villages, constitute the ward level seed committee, typically made up of about 12 members. (A ward consists of six or more villages, each with about 100 households. Thus a ward has about 600 households.) The elected committee in each project area performs tasks such as seed selection and distribution, organizing collective labour at various peak periods, field days, farmers' feedback workshops and training programmes. The responsibility for identifying farmers to multiply and improve seed is also done by the ward committees in collaboration with the local project co-ordinators. An average of six farmers per project site is selected to multiply the preferred seed of the various crop cultivars.

Germplasm exploration and collection expeditions are designed to collect as much genetic diversity as possible. The collection missions are planned jointly by scientists, farmers, farmers' organizations, agriculture extension officers and other interested individuals. Germplasm material is collected throughout the country from farmers' fields, backyards, threshing grounds, farmers' storage facilities and agricultural shows.

The linkage between scientists, farmers and NGOs is of great importance as it provides the necessary dialogue among the three parties involved and offers the opportunity to understand the value of the crop characteristics which are considered important to each group. During the collection expeditions, farmers are consulted and their knowledge and experience documented as background information, together with the common names of each sample collected and details of the area from which it was collected – the passport data. In general, random sampling is practised, which ensures that most of the genetic variation in the population is collected. But farmers' knowledge is also used in identifying distinct features to make sure that characteristics not otherwise included are secured.

All germplasm material is checked for insect damage and purity, registered, cleaned by hand and fumigated. The sample is divided into three equal subsamples for active, medium and long-term storage. All data related to each accession are carefully recorded. Preliminary in-field characterization of the germplasm material consists of recording those characters which are highly heritable and which are expressed in all environments. The exercise is done using the standard germplasm descriptors developed by the International Board for Plant Genetic Resources (IBPGR) and the International Crops Research Institute for the Semi-Arid Tropics (ICRISAT). The characters recorded include: seedling vigour, time of flowering and maturity, plant height, ear length and width, lodging, and other agronomic characters. Further evaluation is done the following season, taking into account the interests of the farmers.

Farmers benefit from the exposure to an array of different varieties of maize, sorghum and pearl millet. During the process, they are able to select material which might have been extinct locally or highly adaptive to their environment. On-farm conservation involves active participation of farmers through all stages of cultivation, selection and storage of folkseed. The farmers' contribution in maintaining genetic diversity is assured through the cultivation of local crop cultivars, including those introduced from elsewhere. Germplasm material collected from similar ecogeographic areas is introduced in areas where the material has been extinct. Farmers' knowledge and experience regarding their local crops are maintained, encouraged and enhanced through information exchange between established farmers' groups.

Seed improvement through selection is undertaken to improve quality. Facilities have been constructed to allow for farmers' easy access to seed at the local level. Duplicate material is then transported to Harare from all project sites for central conservation. The seed is stored as reserves, in case of drought or other calamities. For off-farm conservation, duplicates of all collected germplasm material are kept for long-term storage. These will not be used as routine sources but as security against losses. Given that the seed bank is not yet constructed, jars are used for the purpose. The method ensures that all folkseeds being replaced or threatened by hybrids have representative samples conserved for future use. The permanent seed bank will be built as soon as resources allow.

The seed multiplication component of the project is undertaken in all project sites. The exercise is aimed at ensuring continuous availability of good quality local seed stocks within the communities. Crop cultivars multiplied are those with preferred overall agronomic characteristics. Agronomic trials are undertaken every summer with the objective of determining the characteristics of crop varieties under various conditions, particularly under different fertilizer regimes. The information gathered from the agronomic trials is an important factor in determining the potential of a particular crop variety. Three examples of folkseed and one hybrid of each crop are used in each project site. Trial sites are selected from within the farmer's field to be representative of the area with respect to soil type. Planting starts as soon as possible after the rains, usually mid-November or early December. Harvesting begins when the plants are mature and have dried out. The dates of all the important events, that is, planting, thinning, fertilizer application, time of flowering and maturity, are recorded in the trial dairy. General information based on observations of soil moisture, disease, germination and lodging rates, amongst other factors, is also recorded.

Communication is helped by means of field days and farmers' workshops. At least one field day per season is carried out by ENDA in order to expose farmers to the results of the on-farm trials and to get their feedback according to crop performance evaluation. About a thousand people attend each field day, including the minister or officials from the Ministry of Lands, Agriculture and Rural Resettlement, agricultural extension officers, local administrators, political and party leaders, farmers' and rural development organization representatives, as well as those of other NGOs and the local community. At the field day, farmers describe the operations and management of the trial. The participants assess the performance of different crop varieties under study. The assessment is directed towards the agronomy trial plot, particularly the different fertility levels and crop variety performance. In addition to this, one farmers' workshop is conducted in each of the five project sites every season. At the workshops farmers, scientists and other project staff have an opportunity collectively to review the activities of the project.

Links between the organizing NGOs are important. ZSAN holds bi-monthly meetings to discuss the work of the Indigenous Seeds Project. ZSAN is composed of four indigenous Zimbabwean NGOs: Manicaland Development Association, Silveira House, the Organization for Rural Associations for Progress and ENDA-Zimbabwe. ENDA provides the secretariat. The network meetings provide opportunities to discuss and share experience on food security issues and explore ways of increasing the organizations' co-operation. Some of the items discussed include the national food security situation and its social, cultural and political expressions within the communities. Research approaches and methodologies are collectively criticized and standardized. Information and progress reports of the network members' on-going programmes are exchanged, commented upon and suggestions forwarded, where necessary.

Priorities for the future

The seed improvement programme should be continued and expanded beyond the present pilot study areas. A technical manual for seed improvement methods needs to be developed so that the necessary information on all the techniques is readily at hand. The improvement programme should be part of a wider effort to promote sustainable farming systems as alternatives to highly capital-intensive agriculture. Demonstration plots in selected areas to expose farmers to different sustainable agricultural practices would form a useful contribution to this. The lessons learned from these should be diffused to all interested organizations and farming communities. In support of such work, a Zimbabwean map indicating the areas of genetic diversity and sampling of the material should be produced, and a database of all collected and stored germplasm material established.

Further research is required to assess the viability of establishing a farmer-based seed supply system. Studies should identify the structural framework, management skills and training required, and assess the economic viability of such approaches. Farming systems research could make a useful contribution to assessing the sustainability of agriculture in the semi-arid areas of the country. The study should identify and examine current practices, their successes and limitations, and the scope for improving sustainable farming systems.

There is a broad need for NGO interventions in the field of food security. NGOs are better placed in terms of implementing food security projects at the household level than many government institutions because they are flexible, less bureaucratic, and have the ability to respond to crises. As they operate largely at the grassroots level they are more responsive to local needs. There are immense possibilities for NGOs to collaborate among themselves, and with the government and other institutions, on food security issues. Amongst themselves, NGOs in the region should exchange information and research findings, and share experiences to avoid replication of mistakes and wasting of resources, and to promote successful policies.

8 Ethiopia: a genebank working with farmers

MELAKU WOREDE*

Ethiopia is one of the world's richest centres of crop genetic diversity for many important agricultural plants. It is also being strongly hit by the plague of genetic erosion. The Ethiopian genebank staff are pioneering a national plant genetic resources strategy that marries on-farm conservation and crop improvement at the grassroots level with training, technical support and back-up assistance from the formal sector. Further co-ordination with NGOs will be necessary to avoid contradictions and strengthen national efforts to achieve food security.

The wide range of agroclimatic conditions of the Ethiopian region accounts for its enormous diversity of biological resources. Probably the most important of these resources is the immense range of crop plants grown in the country. Farmers' indigenous landraces, their wild relatives and weedy species, which form the basis of the country's plant genetic resources, are highly prized the world over for their potential value as sources of important genetic characteristics for crop improvement. Among the most important traits which are believed to exist in these materials are earliness, disease and pest resistance, nutritional quality, resistance to drought and other stress conditions, and a host of characteristics especially useful in low input agriculture. Their conservation and development is therefore a prerequisite to the food and livelihood security of the country.

Genetic resources activities already represent a major national effort which the country has systematically undertaken for a decade, but major challenges remain. There is a

* Dr Melaku Worede is director of the Plant Genetic Resources Centre Ethiopia (PGRC/E) which includes the Ethiopian genebank. In 1989 he was granted the Right Livelihood Award (the alternative Nobel Prize) for his outstanding work in promoting sound strategies for genetic resources conservation. He is currently Chairman of the UN Food and Agriculture Organisation's (FAO) Commission on Plant Genetic Resources.

unique and vital opportunity to salvage and to utilize effectively landraces which the farming community has developed and maintained since time immemorial and which at present provide a major part of the existing crop genetic resources in the country.

Past and present efforts made by various scientists to document the country's flora and fauna support the view that the region, because of its wide range of agro-ecological conditions, is the genetic home of a vast number of plant and animal species. Perhaps the most important of these contributions is that of the Russian scientist N.I. Vavilov, who in the late 1920s made a systematic survey to study the country's crop diversity. Based on this survey, Vavilov indicated that the region is an important primary or secondary centre of domestication and diversification for some 38 crops.[1]

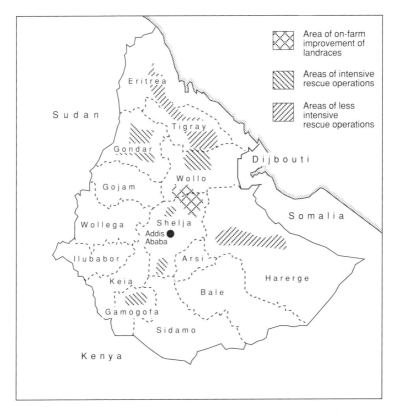

Figure 5. *Map of Ethiopia showing the main areas of activity of the Plant Genetics Resources Centre*

Table 8.1: Estimate of crop diversity in Ethiopia (Adopted from Mengesha, 1975)

Region	Teff	Barley	Sorghum	Wheat	Finger millet	Faba bean	Field pea	Chick pea	Lentil	Grass pea	Fenu-greek	Coffee	Noug
Arsi	L	H	M	H	–	H	M	M	L	T	L	–	T
Bale	L	H	L	H	–	M	M	L	L	–	L	T	–
Eritrea	H	M	H	H	M	M	M	M	L	M	M	T	T
Game Gofa	T	M	H	L	L	M	L	T	L	–	–	M	T
Gojam	H	H	L	M	H	H	H	H	M	H	M	T	H
Gonder	H	M	M	M	H	H	H	H	H	H	H	T	M
Harerge	L	M	H	L	L	M	L	M	L	M	M	H	T
Illubabor	L	L	H	T	L	L	T	–	–	–	–	H	T
Kefa	L	L	M	T	T	L	T	–	–	–	–	H	T
Shewa	H	H	H	H	T	H	H	H	H	M	M	L	H
Sidamo	L	L	L	T	T	L	L	M	–	–	–	H	–
Tigre	H	H	H	M	M	M	M	M	M	M	M	–	M
Welega	M	L	H	H	M	M	–	–	–	M	H	M	–
Welo	H	M	H	M	T	H	H	H	H	M	H	T	M

H, M and L represent high, average and low diversity, respectively; T represents appearance and – represents no data.

Source: Abebe Demissie, PGRC/E, 1989 (Unpublished data).

80

Various other scientists have reported in later expeditions the existence of many cultivated crops which show considerable genetic diversity, and that some of the variations which exist are rare and may not be found elsewhere.[2]

These studies, however, did not fully address the broad wealth of the country's crop plant diversity, partly because expeditions were either sporadic or limited to more accessible areas. Current efforts at documenting the national flora are far more comprehensive and are undertaken on the basis of systematic collecting and scientific studies of a relatively wide range of plants covering different ecological zones of the country. Based on the surveys and explorations made over the last ten years, the PGRC/E has compiled a crop diversity list which provides an estimate of the relative size and distribution of some of the major cultivated crops. It currently covers 98 plant species.

Genetic erosion

The country's broad genetic diversity, particularly that of farmers' landraces and wild relatives, is presently subject to serious and irreversible erosion, which is progressing at an alarming rate. Of the various factors involved the most important are: replacement of indigenous landraces by new, genetically uniform crop varieties; changes and developments in agriculture or land use; destruction of habitats; and drought. These are discussed below with due account given to some of the steps being undertaken to minimize their impact on the country's genetic resources.

Displacement of native cultivars
Ongoing conservation of the existing variability in crop species is partly attributed to the traditional farming systems in regions of high diversity. Farmers, consciously or unconsciously, have been maintaining highly heterogeneous populations of seed stock for many generations. Traditional farming allowed for the continued co-existence of cultivated crops species and their wild relatives. These often intercrossed, thereby generating new variations. The situation is now changing, however, as the normally lower-yielding cultivars are being displaced by new improved varieties and, in certain instances, by other crops.

Not all crops, however, are affected in the same way and to

the same degree. Native barleys, for example, are suffering major losses as they are being replaced by other crops, particularly introduced wheat varieties. Farmers are growing more bread wheat as a result of increased market demand and also because of the availability of high-yielding varieties (HYVs) which can be grown in the high-altitude zones traditionally planted to barley. Durum wheat is giving way to new bread varieties, especially in relatively well-developed regions like Arsi and, to a lesser degree, Ada in the Central Highlands, where there have been extensive wheat breeding activities since the late 1960s. Cultivation of locally developed teff (*Eragrostis tef*), though, appears also to be expanding due to high demand and to the adaptability of this crop to waterlogged soil conditions under which many other crops fail to grow. Improved varieties, therefore, are not a threat to this crop since they succumb to disease and pest problems.

Similarly, with sorghum and millet, exot' varieties do not pose any immediate threat as expansion of such material is at present restricted. In the case of sorghum, however, genetic erosion is occurring, due to extensive selection within the native populations themselves, which is narrowing their base of genetic diversity. A similar situation exists also with the various pulses, legumes and oil crops grown, where the bulk of the material used in breeding programmes is represented by indigenous landraces.

Loss of wild genepools through habitat destruction
Another important threat to the country's genetic resources is changes in land use or advances in agriculture, which often result in the disappearance of habitats containing important wild genetic resources. Seven-eighths of forest cover had already vanished by the mid-1960s, but the present situation is even worse, as forest continues to be cleared for the expansion of agriculture and as a result of other pressures of a rapidly growing population. Much of the large tracts of grazing land, important sites for wild and weedy relatives of major food and fibre crops, are threatened by the plough as a result of the pressure to meet the growing food shortages in the country.

The effects of drought
Drought often results in genetic erosion as a result of poor growing conditions, either by selective elimination of

particular genotypes in the crop or by total crop failure. The latter can amount to genetic wipe-out of the variety concerned. This is particularly likely under rainfed conditions, where moisture stresses prevail. With backyard crops like vegetables, the problem is not so severe except in those villages suffering extreme drought.

The indirect effects of drought can be just as important. The droughts of recent years have sometimes forced farmers to eat their own seed supply in order to survive, or to sell their stored seed as a food commodity. In these cases, there can be a massive displacement of native seed stocks as farmers try to plant the grains introduced as food aid by relief agencies.

To try and match this threat, PGRC/E has launched a Seed Reserve Programme in collaboration with the Ethiopian Seed Corporation, in the principal areas suffering from recurring drought. Also, since 1987 the centre has concentrated its germplasm rescue operations in these areas, mainly in the central and northeastern regions of the country.

Impact of current breeding initiatives

Despite their value as sources of resistance to pests and diseases and of other adaptive characters, some traditional cultivars or landraces are relatively low yielding, or may have no immediate value as varieties in their own right. In many developing countries, breeders are therefore compelled to resort to higher-yielding cultivars, especially in situations where land is scarce and food shortages exist. These can be introduced as planting material or used in local breeding programmes to improve the yield of local types.

In the national crop improvement programme, improved or introduced varieties are always compared to established varieties, which usually include locally adapted types. This, to some degree, acts as a check against releasing introduced varieties if better local ones already exist. However, even this check can be biased against the indigenous genetic resources since the local type used in the check might not be representative of the huge potential which exists in the country. One way to counter this problem is to improve the performance of traditional varieties. The durum wheat landrace improvement programme is an example of this vital step towards resolving this problem.

The role of farmers in genetic resources conservation

The need for timely action to salvage Ethiopia's still-abundant biological resources led to the setting up of the PGRC/E in 1976. The centre's genebank was developed from previous holdings of crop germplasm at various breeding and scientific institutions. The genebank presently holds over 50,000 accessions of some 100 crop species comprising indigenous landraces repatriated from other national programmes, as well as those collected directly from the field. More than 115 collecting missions have been undertaken in the last 14 years, in all regions, covering a broad range of crop types and agro-ecological systems. Priority has been given to those species of greatest social and economic importance which are most threatened by genetic erosion, whether from the expansion of new varieties, natural disasters or changes in land use. A significant improvement in conservation policies is the increased involvement of farmers in the collection exercise.

As in many developing countries, farmers play a central role in the conservation of genetic resources since they are holding the bulk of those resources. Unless circumstances prove impossible, small-scale farmers alway retain some seed stock for security. Even when forced to leave their farms temporarily because of severe drought, farmers store small quantities of seed in clay pots or similar containers, which they seal and bury in a safe place on the farm so that they can come back a few years later to reclaim and use them. Throughout the country, farmers have also established networks to facilitate seed supply, including the exchange of seeds through local markets. This provides an assortment of crop types with a wide range of adaptability.

In these ways, farmers have access to a wide choice of planting material. Seed which is unsuitable under certain conditions can be stored for use in a more appropriate planting season. In regions which are becoming more developed, like the Central Highlands, such practices are less and less common, as new varieties are introduced. But in most of the drought-prone areas, like Northern Shewa and Welo, farmers continue to rely on these systems.

Ethiopian farmers have also played a key role in the creation, maintenance and promotion of crop genetic diversity through a series of activities which they have developed over centuries to sustain crop productivity. In many small-scale farms around the country, cultivated crops often inter-cross with their wild and weedy relatives which are growing in the same field or nearby, resulting in plants with new characteristics. Farmers have long taken advantage of this process, adapting such new plants to meet agronomic realities. Similarly, use of mixtures and inter-cropping has often resulted in rapid diversification through accidental crosses amongst different species of a crop. This process of introgression is believed to be the origin of new types of *Brassica* species observed on farms where *B. carinata* (Ethiopian mustard) and *B. nigra* (Black mustard) are grown in mixtures.

In order to improve crop security, local varieties of coffee are planted by farmers along the edges of the fields sown to the more uniform lines distributed by the Coffee Improvement Project. This way, their farms are active field genebanks. This is a tremendous input to the genetic resources centre's efforts to maintain genetic resources in the field, especially since it is difficult to store coffee seed safely on a long-term basis. The centre has also benefited from the knowledge and skills of farming families in collaborating in its activities, especially in the collection and identification of useful plant material.

Given the inherent advantages of traditional practices, on-farm landrace conservation and enhancement provides a valuable option for conserving genetic diversity. It also offers a mechanism for continued evolution of plant characteristics and the on-going generation of new variability. This is especially significant in regions susceptible to drought, because it is under those environmental extremes that adaptation to stress occurs. Similarly, for pest and disease resistance, continued host-parasite co-evolution can go on. There is an outstanding need to maintain landraces growing under field conditions for use in crop improvement programmes, and this is probably best achieved through farm- or community-based conservation programmes.

The centre's approach: on-farm diversity

On-farm conservation and enhancement of landraces has been an aspect of the PGRC/E's work since 1988, involving farmers, scientists and extension workers. The rationale behind the community-based approaches promoted by the

Table 8.2: PGRC/E on-farm landrace conservation and enhancement sites in northeastern Shewa and southeastern Wello districts (1989–90 crop year)

Region	Sub-district	Locality	Crop type	No. of hectares	Crop harvest Q/ha
Northeast Shewa	Efratana Jille	Merewa Hadre	Nech Teff	1	8
	Efratana Jille	Laygnaw Ataye	Nech Teff	2	16
			Sorghum	2	50
	Efratana Jille	Laygnaw Ataye	Sorghum	1	25
	Efratana Jille	Saramba	Sorghum	2	50
	Efratana Jille	Hora Dildaye	Sorghum	1	25
	Efratana Jille	Allala Kubeya	Nech Teff	1	8
			Sorghum	1	25
	Efratana Jille	Ataye[1]	Sorghum	1	25
	Kore Meda	Kore Meda	Sorghum	1	25
	Efratana Timuga	Majette	Abolse Teff	2	16
	Efratana Timuga	Gemza	Abolse Teff	3	24
	Fursi	Jarra	Sorghum	1	25

Region	Sub-district	Locality	Crop type	No. of hectares	Crop harvest Q/ha
Southeast Wello	Cheffa	Addis Mendir	Sorghum	2	50
	Kallu	Kedidda	Sorghum	2	50
	Batti	Birra	Sorghum	1	25
	Batti	Salmene	Peas	1	10
	Artuma	Cherettee	Chick pea	1	10
			Sorghum	2	50
			Nech Teff	2	16
	Esseye Gella	Kamisse	Corn	2	40
	Dessie Zuria	02 Kellina	Fesho Teff	2	16
	Dessie Zuria	Gerado 01	Nech Bungne Teff	2	16
			Peas	1	10
	Dessie Zuria	Gerado 05	Fesho Teff	1	8

1) Also used as a demonstration site.

Source: Hailu Getu, USC/C.

Table 8.3: List of major cultivars (races/sub-races) of sorghum (*Bicolor bicolor*) traditionally grown by peasant farmers in south-east Wello and northeast Shewa, currently utilized in the landrace conservation project

Race	Local name* (sub-race)	Main usage	Special characteristics of local importance
Durra (D)	Wotet Begunche/D-22	Local bread (Enjera)	High lysine sorghum
Durra (D)	Goronojo chibit/D-2	Local bread (Enjera)	High lysine sorghum, bird resistant
Durra (D)	Key degalit	Local bread (Enjera)	Bird resistant
Durra (D)	Abdelot netch/D-10	Local beer	
Durra (D)	Chibite Wagare/D-9	Local bread	Bird resistant, drought tolerant
Durra (D)	Ambasel Zengada/D-5	Local bread	Bird resistant
Durra (D)	Abdelot key/D-11	Local beer	
Durra (D)	Bicha mantu/D-19	Local beer	
Durra (D)	Derb Keteto/D-20	Local bread	Bird resistant
Durra (D)	Bicha marchuke/D-24	Local beer	
Durra (D)	Netch marchuke/D-25	Local bread	
Guinea caudatum (GC)	Alengua/GC-1	Local beer	
Guinea caudatum (GC)	Ganga/GC-2	Local bread	

Race	Local name* (sub-race)	Main usage	Special characteristics of local importance
Caudatum (C)	Gobe adi/C-1	Local bread	
Caudatum (C)	Sibesibe cherekit/C-3		
Caudatum (C)	Shotate cherekit/C-2		
Durra bicolor (DB)	Mishinga warrabessa/DB-6	Local bread	High lysine sorghum
Durra caudatum (DC)	Keredebia/DC-1	Local beer	Drought tolerant
Durra bicolor (DB)	Fendisha/DB-7		
Durra (D)	Dogongof/D-6	Local beer	Bird resistant
Durra (D)	Wagare netch/D-7	Local bread	Drought tolerant
Durra (D)	Wagare key/D-8	Local beer	Bird resistant
Durra (D)	Netch Kondale/D-4	Local bread	
Durra (D)	Muyera netch/D-12	Local bread	
Durra (D)	Bitin manta/D-18	Local beer	
Guinea caudatum (GC)	Zera-Zera/GC-3	Local bread	

centre is to encourage farmers to maintain landrace varieties by improving the genetic performance of them. Two basic approaches are employed: assisting farmers in mass selection to improve their landrace varieties; and developing and maintaining élite landraces on the farm. In each case, farmers' fields act not only as sources of planting material but also as field genebanks for a wider range of landraces which, while not of immediate agronomic value as varieties, are used in evaluating selections and as a depository of useful genetic characteristics.

Varieties developed from locally adapted landraces could also serve as the check in national yield trials and thus help restrain the expansion of high risk seeds. Instead of using introduced varieties, farmers are provided with élite populations of improved versions of more adapted local types. This is especially valuable for areas characterized by marginal growing conditions or environmental extremes where conventional improved varieties are less likely to meet the needs of farmers.

On-farm improvement of landraces by mass selection

Programmes to assist farmers in the improvement of landraces by mass selection are being consolidated within a network of farms at strategic sites in northeast Shewa and southeast Welo through support provided by the Unitarian Service Committee of Canada (USC/C). The farmers, mostly women, are organized through their respective farming co-operatives. They have access to the genetic resources of the centre's genebank, representing material from all over Ethiopia, and PGRC/E scientists assist the farmers in their programmes of mass selection, which improves landrace productivity season by season.

Selection is usually carried out at heading time, when many of the distinctions among the various plant types become visible. Types are selected for important characteristics such as pest and disease resistance, size of kernel/head, earliness and other criteria of local importance. The farmers make their selections based on their judgement and long-established skills. Additionally, farmers will rogue, or pull out, plants which already show signs of disease or other negative effects. The seeds of plants finally selected are harvested. A new, somewhat improved population is used as the future seed supply after multiplication. This is the basis of mass selection; selection might continue to be carried out in following years for further improvement. After about three to five seasons of selection and multiplication, an appreciable degree of improvement in crop yield would be expected. It is at this stage that it can be worthwhile to cross with genetic materials from external sources, which contain characteristics of interest.

Farmers also undertake critical evaluations of their selections by comparing their performance with representative samples of the original seed stock planted alongside. These plantings also contribute to on-farm conservation of the original landrace material. Certain types of cultivars which might otherwise be abandoned for various reasons, such as low-yield or marketing problems, are already being conserved this way.

On-farm development and maintenance of élite landrace selections

Another aspect in landrace conservation and utilization by farmers is the maintenance and development of élite indigenous landrace selections on-farm. This takes the farmer-scientist link one stage further and is a slight modification of conventional mass selection. The programme is undertaken jointly between the PGRC/E and the Debre Zeit Research Centre of the Alemaya University of Agriculture with finance from USC/C, and uses wheat germplasm collected by the centre over the last seven years.

The approach involves selecting pure lines adapted to different environmental stresses. After yield testing and bulking of two or more superior lines, the élite material is further multiplied and distributed to farmers. Preliminary yield trials have shown that the performance of a few élite landrace selections developed in this way surpasses those of commercially released varieties.

Farmers are involved by multiplying and using the élite seed stock provided by the breeder, while the centre maintains representative samples in long-term storage in the gene-bank. The approach allows the farmers to continue to use their landrace varieties, ensuring effective use of the superior germplasm without any threat of losing the indigenous population. The centre gives advice on all aspects related to conservation, use and distribution of the material, while the local USC/C agent provides technical guidance on seed production and multiplication.

Linking conservation and use

The value of landraces to farmers in developing countries is only realized if they can be used as a dependable source of planting material. It is vital, therefore, that enhanced seed are multiplied for distribution, to maximize their use on the farm. It may make very little sense to conserve landraces unless the systems are in place to multiply, produce, distribute and deliver to farmers materials developed from these sources.

The best way to achieve this is probably through community-based seed production, marketing and distribution systems operating in networks, perhaps by enhancing or further organizing the traditional networks which were described earlier. Through this approach, farmers will be able to control the choice of varieties, and will have ready access to planting material adapted to local growing conditions. They will also be in a position to evaluate critically the relative performance of a wide range of varieties.

The practice of maintaining landraces on-farm may be limited by the relative low yield of such materials. However, farmers do recognize the advantages of stability and adaptation to local growing conditions, and are often reluctant to adopt new seeds. The enhancement of landraces and research to promote their effectiveness may, therefore, benefit farmers by offering a compromise between yield and stability. In some marginal growing conditions and extreme environments, landraces may even provide a more valuable option than introduced varieties.

Future co-operation with NGOs

A growing international network of NGOs is involved in community approaches to plant genetic resource conservation as part of the rural development programmes they are supporting. Their activities range from such short-term relief operations as the provision of food resources, including seeds, farming tools and oxen, to longer-term projects which are designed to increase food production and environmental conservation in drought-prone areas.

The agencies recognize the central importance of indigenous genetic resources for the food and livelihood security of the country's growing population. For many of the crops grown, local landraces will continue to be the main planting material and provide the genetic resource base for plant breeding programmes. It is vital for the success of such programmes on the conservation and sustainable use of genetic resources that their activities are integrated with those of farming and community organizations, professional organizations and government agencies. The PGRC/E will continue to assist in co-ordinating these activities and to exploit opportunities to promote genetic resource conservation and use as part of the aid agencies' activities.

Many of these activities could be re-oriented to include genetic resource conservation and use in overall programmes geared to the sustainable management of natural resources by local communities. The following activities might be considered for integration into development projects:

○ The *in situ* conservation of wild relatives of cultivated crop species and of wild species of potential value could be included as part of community grazing-land development and management programmes. Such land could be further developed through the incorporation of selected indigenous grass and legume species (local, or from other regions).

○ Community seed banks or genetic gardens of locally adapted species, including enhanced landraces, could be set up to provide a sustainable supply of planting material and reduce dependency on introduced varieties.

○ Endangered plant species, and especially economically and ecologically critical species, could be planted as part of community-managed environmental rehabilitation schemes. There are several wild trees, shrubs and grasses which communities traditionally use as food resources, for medicinal purposes and as fuel could be integrated into such a scheme.

These activities should be undertaken in co-operation with local people who are in the best position to identify the species and varieties of interest to them. The centre and other relevant scientific institutions could provide guidance and monitoring on technical aspects of the conservation work. Seminars and workshops could be organized to stimulate awareness of the need for conservation and to encourage and sustain action at the local level. They should involve local extension agents, scientific institutions and NGO field officials as well as rural communities and schools.

The integration of genetic resources conservation activities into agency-supported development projects is a challenging task which requires co-ordination at national and local levels in order to achieve a rational use of staff and infrastructural resources, and to harmonize conservation with development. Presently, there appear to exist some gaps between project NGOs engaged in rural development work and the community genetic resource activities co-ordinated by the centre. Some seed multiplication, storage and distribution activities of NGOs appear to be disjointed and not co-ordinated with the activities of the centre, for example.

The PGRC/E will continue to direct its efforts to increase the involvement of farmers in the conservation and utilization of the country's genetic resources to cover a broader range of sites and agro-ecological conditions. In the long run, *in situ* conservation of the wild relatives of crops and other valuable plants growing on grazing and range lands, as well as animal genetic resources, will be integrated into the programme.

A wide range of root and tuber crops. Local control of production of planting material ensures that this diversity is maintained.

Local markets in South America display an impressive diversity of vegetables. A wide range of types and varieties are still demanded.

A potato farmer in Ecuador. Local farmers grow an impressive range of traditional varieties, often alongside introduced ones.

9 Developing local seed production in Mozambique

ANDREA GAIFAMI*

Beyond the necessary conservation of genetic resources, it is important to meet farmers' needs for quality seed in adequate quantities. Local seed companies, in which both farmers and the government participate, are a difficult but important challenge to take up in order to strengthen indigenous farming systems through a locally controlled seed industry.

Locally controlled seed production is an important component of rural farming systems, which can be credible alternatives to large-scale, industrialized forms of agricultural production. Control over seeds is vital to meet the real needs of local markets, and to protect farmers' knowledge of traditional varieties. But if local seed production is to be sustainable, it must also be economically viable. This is why Crocevia has found it important to help establish local seed companies in developing countries, often as a mixture between a private enterprise and a government agency. Small development project agencies can help local non-governmental organizations (NGOs) by supporting aspects of seed production which are not profitable in themselves, that is the collection, evaluation and conservation of genetic material.

In small-scale farming regions of many developing countries, the large majority of seeds are still produced by the farmers themselves. This in itself is a good sign. It shows that the peasant farmer culture is well-rooted in the country and can offer the necessary knowledge to maintain a productive cycle based on the reproduction of seeds, using very simple techniques and know-how. But seed supply is only one of the

* Andrea Gaifami, an Italian agronomist, is the Coordinator of the Agriculture Programme of the Centro Internazionale Crocevia, based in Rome. For the past several years, he has been actively participating in the various projects Crocevia supports that have a strong emphasis on the conservation and use of local genetic diversity in Africa, Asia and Latin America.

Figure 6 *Map of Mozambique showing the location of the Niassa Local Seeds Enterprise*

basic requirements for agricultural production, and better seeds are demanded by most farmers. Without downgrading the techniques which have, over the centuries, generated the improvements and adaptability of the local varieties cultivated by peasant farmers, greater demands have to be met. Setting up local companies specialized in seed production can help meet those demands through economies of scale and developing the expertise to produce quality seed for local farming.

The rationale for local seed enterprises

The seeds market in Mozambique, for example, is still quite virgin and will certainly attract foreign seed companies in a matter of time. Given the widespread links of such companies to agrochemicals, and their capacities for mass distribution, this could eventually result in economic damage to the country and the disappearance of local varieties and indigenous ecotypes. Already, some crop species are being marginalized and are disappearing from the commercial circuits, because they do not justify the research and development costs, according to the criteria of multinationals in the seed sector. Large-scale, high-tech agriculture necessarily needs to be part of a large-scale market, using varieties which are adapted, or accepted, by a large number of farmers covering huge extensions of land. The most relevant share of marketed seeds in Mozambique is maize, while the more traditional national crops are disappearing slowly, and have never, in fact, really been present on the seed market.

Local seed production must be considered a valid alternative to the subsidiaries of transnational corporations (TNCs). The establishment of a company with strong local roots and serving local markets also recognizes the value of economically minor species and can serve those needs. Local seed enterprises must have a solid economic base in order to counterbalance effectively the overwhelming capacity of large companies to occupy any market share which might appear. But while small-scale production units should be locally controlled, and oriented to satisfy local needs and standards, they cannot avoid national laws and economic realities if they are to be really sustainable rather than permanently dependent on external finances or emergency hand-outs. However, activities which are not profitable on a short-term basis can and must be supported by external funds.

In the medium term, local companies might generate an economic return from seed sales, as well as from other similar products: young trees, grafts, tubers, roots or vegetative materials, and products derived from test trials. This, in turn, could promote further investment, enhancing rural development and reducing the normal flow of local capital to the cities. Similarly, the creation of farmers' co-operatives could promote the development of seed production activities. In these cases, support from foreign NGOs could provide the investment for the initial infrastructural foundation of such farmer-based activities.

Like any other activity, seed production has economic, social and political facets, not to mention ecological considerations. The first aim of local seed production should be to meet local needs. Generally speaking, that implies a small and marginal market share. But that does not mean that local companies working in small markets are immune to pressure from multinationals. Seed enterprises in developing countries which are purely privately owned might be more easily subject to being taken over by large companies as part of the concentration process the world seed industry is undergoing. Recently, Pioneer took control of minor Zimbabwean companies, while Cargill bought the Malawian Seed Company. Attempts have been made by some firms to enter Mozambique as well.

Local governments should be responsible for strategic planning of the seed sector. Their presence in the direct management of small seed-production units is desirable, as this would represent their concrete interest in the development of small rural industries as well as helping to guarantee their commercial independence. However, it can be a fatal error to allow political interference in day-to-day management of seed production. The political experience of administrators, governmental technicians or local clerks is distinct from managerial ability. While political objectives could, and must, determine medium- and long-term plans, economic accountability through a balance sheet has to be prepared at the end of the year.

Conservation must not be neglected, of course. At the grassroots level, special care must be taken to develop the proper balance, or compromise, between collection, conservation and production. Effective germplasm collection requires access to specific areas and the co-operation of local people who should be positively involved. Local conservation activities should support seed production. A museum-like logic of pure conservation of genetic diversity should be left to those institutions financed to carry out such work.

Finally, any foreign-funded programme has to foresee the future viability of the action implemented. In the case of seed production it means a system must be provided for an economic return to guarantee the independence of breeders, sellers, administrative managers and field inspectors employed in the company. There would be no sense in establishing new structures, with great potential strategic interest, if their activities cannot be guaranteed with a certain degree of security.

Crocevia's experience in Niassa

The foregoing illustrates the advantage of establishing a seed company as a 'social business', a mixture of private and public interests which correspond at the time to what meets the various and specific requirements of the area best. For example, in the isolated Niassa province of Mozambique, a mixed company, the *Gabinete de Produçao de Sementes do Niassa* (GPSN) was set up. This fits in with the Economic Recovery Plan of the Mozambican government, which calls upon all economic operators in the country to get closer in line with daily financial realities. Indiscriminate and uncontrolled assistance to the state companies has ceased, giving way to private enterprise, which is growing in the areas being abandoned by the large government-run projects. At the same time, the crucial and highly strategic importance of seeds means that they cannot be left in the hands of private interests alone.

The GPSN has a central role in seed production and distribution, as well as in co-ordinating the activities of farmers and public and private companies, according to an agreed policy framework. It also channels credit and technical assistance. However, the seed multiplication system involves many institutions at various levels. The National and Provincial Directorates of Agriculture are responsible for overall policy on rural development. Pre-basic and basic seed is produced by the National Institute of Agricultural Research, while the National Seeds Service is responsible for quality control and certification. Credits are provided by the Provincial Rural Development Bank. Seed multiplication is carried out by farmers through contracts with seed companies, private, public and co-operatives. The identification of suitable companies and the drawing up of the contracts is done by the GPSN.

Crocevia is involved in the team which directs GPSN. The major shareholder in GPSN is the state-owned company *Sementes do Moçambique Limitada* (SEMOC) which represents the interests of the Department of Agriculture. SEMOC provides assistance in accounting, setting up contracts and staff training for GPSN.

Experience in neighbouring countries of southern Africa had already shown that it was not feasible for a seed production and marketing company to cover alone the actual

101

multiplication of the seeds necessary to meet market demand. The organizational structure chosen for GPSN therefore was one of a network of technical assistance to farmers who multiply seeds under contract. Added to this is the logistical assistance to provide companies or private contractors with the necessary production factors and equipment not ordinarily available on the local market. The strategy of contracting out the multiplication work allows farmers to contribute their knowledge to seed production and helps promote the distribution of good agricultural techniques, and does away with the need to locate seed multiplication sites in one defined area, thus avoiding many phytosanitary problems; in addition, it facilitates the production of seeds which are well adapted to the environments in which they will be used.

GPSN plays a central role in facilitating credit accession for farmers or contract growers. It is important that the company provides the link between the bank and seed producers, since credit to small farmers would otherwise often be restricted. The company can ask for major credit which is then passed on to the farmers or used for central purchasing of necessary inputs.

The structure of GPSN and its links with governmental organizations allows local seed production to be integrated with national programmes. This is vital in order to reinforce the structural base of the seed company; as well, the parallel institution of a genetic conservation programme can be of the greatest interest. The enterprise needs to have good genetic materials to rely upon, be they samples of local varieties or pre-basic seeds maintained in acceptable conditions. This is particularly true if you suppose that seed production is carried on not only for emergency or shortage problems but to supply people with improved seeds. Furthermore, a national seed conservation programme can include agronomic tests carried out all over the country, the results of which must be known to any seed producer. Reciprocally, any national agricultural research system usually has great difficulties in understanding what real rural conditions are, in many cases due to the negative influences of expatriate researchers or traditional university education. Under those conditions, the best connection between seed research and real customers is the seed company (even better if it is a small company which has direct links with the farmers). These relationships can also favour the seed company in providing

Table 9.1: Plan for home-made production, 1990 Gabinete de Produçao de Sementes do Niassa (GPSN)

Variety	Area (m²)
Sunhemp, green manuring	39,240
Obregon Maize, in ridges	8,350
Maize, post control test and div. varieties	9,050
Maize, basic Obregon	10,500
Amendoim, Makulu red	2,907
Sunhemp, seed	2,150
Sorghum (ex-Chimoio)	846
Sorghum, Tsabatsye	432
Sorghum, Cumbande	36
Okra, Mavago	720
Sorghum, Chigomole	360
Okra, Lago	36
Okra (ex-Zimbabwe)	8
Okra, Clemson spineless	11
Potato, various	1,216
Peanuts, Mawanga	2,000
Bambarra, Amarelo	180
Beans, Manteiga (in ridges)	3,500
Bambarra, Preto	2
Peanuts, Mawanga	4,320
Squash, zucchini	96
Pigeon pea, Amarelo manchado	84
Pigeon pea, Preto	93
Various fodder, IPA test	176
Bambarra, Castanho	60
Soya, Hardee	920
Soya, Oribi	11,400
Peanuts, Mawanga – Basic	360
Maize, Ferke – Basic	500
Lablab	19
Maize, Sarap'ome	252
Maize, Obregon – transplanted	806
Peanuts, red/white – Basic	96
Soya, IAC6	5,618
Sesame	240
Sorghum, Serena – Basic	836
Hyacinth bean, green	836
Soya IAC7	5,850
Hyacinth bean, white	n.a.
Wheat, Kenya Nyati	n.a.
Cassava test, local	160
True Potato Seeds	140
Sweet potato test, local	n.a.
Coriander – Basic	n.a.
Coriander – Seed	n.a.
Okra, Mavago – Basic	n.a.
Okra, Lago – Basic	n.a.
Sunflower, local Malemia	n.a.
Chick pea, local	n.a.

access, through the national institutions, to the international seed germplasm exchange network.

While the project has met with difficulties and has suffered delays, the objectives have been gradually met and the establishment of an autonomous company has effectively challenged the general assumption that Niassa is an area suitable for emergency and basic survival activities only.

The range of crops and varieties handled by GPSN is vast, covering maize, sorghum, wheat, cassava, peanuts, pulses, oilseeds and vegetables (Table 9.1). In terms of the different varieties, the different crops and the different quantities of various seeds, the more direct link between customers and suppliers can stimulate a strong feeling of local participation in the company's development and planning. Could anyone imagine a big seed company maintaining, treating and selling such a range of different varieties?

Benefits and problems

The establishment of the seed company has helped to stimulate local economic activity. The need to enhance the local economy and the role of provincial structures has been an imperative, given the relative isolation of Niassa, exacerbated by the interruption of the railway which connects Niassa with Nampula and Nacala, due to the war. External agricultural inputs are double or triple the price found in other parts of the country. In these regions, local control over seed production assumes a special significance in meeting the particular needs of the zone, by producing seed which requires fewer external inputs. The guerilla war has caused problems for the project too, forcing its reorientation in order to provide a situation of reasonable safety for the staff and for the local people working on the project.

Amongst more general problems is the lack of financial resources in rural areas. It can be very difficult to secure grants for local seed production activities, even though, as medium or long-term programmes, they are not particularly costly. An assurance that funds will not vanish midway is vital. It can also be problematic to attract the good quality technical staff required since educated technicians prefer to settle in the large urban areas.

One of the other main obstacles is the actual acceptance of improved varieties among the farmers. Acceptance may be low, due either to previous bad experiences from hybrid seeds distributed through emergency programmes or because of inadequate information. A useful instrument is the 'field day'. On this occasion, extension workers, administrators, technicians, representatives from the different villages, associations or communities are invited to visit the experimental plot or the basic seed multiplication farm. Reactions can be collected from selected people; reciprocally, the same guests will be informed about the company's production plans, prices and distribution schemes. Usually, the best relations between customers and supplier create greater satisfaction on both sides. An open-door policy always gives good results.

Food aid and other foreign aid schemes can undermine fledgling local seed companies. They have the power to squeeze small local industries out of the market by distribution of free or cheap seeds. This applies particularly to big organizations devoted to emergency aid distribution, which are dominated by urgent needs. In order to withstand these pressures, seed companies should develop the best marketing strategies in order to interact with the customers. At the local level, an information campaign should lead to better diffusion of local products, and a marketing strategy must be carefully planned, based on an understanding of peoples' real needs.

Crocevia's experience in genetic resources management programmes ranges from almost entirely institutional programmes in the Nicaraguan cow milk network to highly decentralized structures such as one project involving 180 families in the Yantenga province of Burkina Faso. It is not possible to say that one method is better than the other. There is only one guiding principle: 'Let the farmers be the managers of their own resources'.

10 Grassroots conservation efforts in Latin America

CAMILA MONTECINOS and MIGUEL ALTIERI*

Peasant agriculture of Latin America has given the world the potato, maize and tomato, and the wild and domesticated forms which are necessary to improve them. But the breeding and conservation efforts of the formal sector do little to address small farmers' needs for sustainable production systems. Over the past years, a range of grassroots approaches to maintaining and using local genetic resources has emerged throughout Latin America, often through the work of non-governmental organizations (NGOs). But the constraints and limitations are huge.

Latin America is an ecologically diverse region and a major repository of biodiversity and genetic resources. It is also a culturally heterogeneous continent with more than 100 ethnic groups still managing ecosystems with indigenous technologies. The continents' farmers, hunters and gatherers manage, maintain and develop genetic resources and in so doing provide ecological and socio-economic services to the world community for the advancement of agriculture, forestry and industry, as well as for the maintenance of the biosphere. Many of these sustainable management systems are increasingly being recognized as useful in guiding modern resource management.

* Camila Montecinos is a Chilean agronomist. She works with the Centro de Educación y Tecnología (CET), an NGO which carries out research and provides technical training on sustainable agriculture and energy to farmers and their organizations throughout the southern half of Chile. Camila is responsible for CET's work in the field of genetic resources. Miguel Altieri, also Chilean, is an agronomist teaching at the University of California in Berkeley. He has published several articles and books on agro-ecology and sustainable agriculture in Latin America. Both Camila and Miguel are active in the Latin American Consortium for Agroecology and Development (CLADES). This chapter is based on the authors' 'Status and Trends in Grassroots Crop Genetic Conservation Efforts in Latin America', a contribution to the WRI/IUCN/UNEP Biodiversity Strategy Programme.

Genetic diversity in traditional farming systems

In Latin America, traditional agro-ecosystems represent centuries of accumulated experience of interaction with the environment of farmers who have not had access to external inputs, capital, credit and developed markets. The farmers use locally available resources to manage farming systems giving sustained yields. Central to these systems is the wide use of genetic resources which promotes diversity of diet and income source, stability of production, reduced pest and disease incidence, and efficient use of labour. Traditional multiple cropping systems are estimated to provide still as much as one-fifth of the region's food supply.[1] Agroforestry systems throughout the American tropics commonly contain well over 100 plant species per field, species used for construction materials, firewood, tools, medicine, livestock feed and human food. In Mexico, for example, Huastec Indians manage over 300 species in agricultural and fallow fields, home gardens and forest plots.

Many traditional agro-ecosystems are located in the Latin American centres of diversity (*viz* Meso-America, the Andes and southern Chile, and the Brazil–Paraguay zone) where wild and weedy relatives of crops exist alongside landraces. The landrace populations consist of mixtures of genetic lines, all of which are well adapted to the region in which they have evolved, but differ in the mechanisms by which they express traits such as pest resistance. Some lines are resistant or tolerant to certain races of pathogens, and some to others. In the Andes, farmers are known to cultivate as many as 50 potato varieties in their fields. The resulting genetic diversity confers at least partial resistance to diseases specific to particular strains of the crop and allows farmers to exploit different microclimates and derive multiple nutritional and other uses from within-species genetic variations.[2]

Wild and weedy relatives of crops often grow throughout a much wider range of ecological conditions than the crops derived from them and therefore have genes giving greater resistance and tolerance to ecological extremes. This feature has been exploited by farmers and professional breeders alike in enhancing the resistance or adaptive range of crops. The International Potato Centre (CIP) in Lima, for example, has 1,450 types of 19 species of wild potatoes for use in its breeding programmes, many collected from traditional farming systems. Within these systems, useful characteristics contained in the wild relatives are transferred by crossing into the landraces, adding to and replenishing their host of useful traits. In Mexico, farmers allow teosinte to grow close to their maize fields so that when the wind pollinates the maize some natural crosses occur which may develop into hybrid plants.[3] This practice can increase yields, and similar procedures are used by farmers for other crops. Farmers manage introgression in order to encourage desirable traits (such as increased pungency in cultivated chilies by hybridization with wild chilepines) and to discourage unwanted crosses (such as a bitter flavour in squashes by contamination from wild gourds). Farmers also use weeds directly for medicinal or flavouring purposes, or for biological pest control, managing weed populations for their beneficial effects while limiting any negative competitive effect on the crop.[4]

Mainenance of species and genetic diversity in fields is one of the effective strategies to create stable systems by resource-poor farmers practising low-input agriculture in marginal environments. The incredible diversity of potato varieties used in traditional Andean farming systems is a case in point. Greatest diversity can be found in the central Andes of southern Peru and northern Bolivia, where 50 to 70 named varieties can be found in a single locality. Diversity is not due to random planting of numerous varieties but is maintained by careful planning, together with controlled systems of potato selection and exchange. For example, major non-bitter potato types are planted in different fields using two types of management system. In fields designed for subsistence food production, planting tends to be of randomly placed mixtures. Seed potatoes for propagation are selected for the quality rather than size. In fields designed for production of potatoes and seed tubers for external markets, more ordered and uniform plantings of native varieties are made. Around both types of field, wild and weedy relatives are allowed to grow, promoting crosses from these sources.

Genetic erosion and trends in conservation

Genetic erosion is a major concern in Latin/America as elsewhere, although there have been few systematic studies as to its real extent. It occurs because farmers, pushed by social, economic and technical forces, change their farming systems and grow more, introduced, high-yielding varieties (HYVs). Farmers, however, still grow native varieties alongside the introduced ones and the spread of HYVs is clearly not evenly distributed between regions, between farmers, or even within a single farm. Adoption of the new technologies is far more advanced on farms in lowland valleys close to urban centres and markets, than in more distant zones, particularly the higher mountainous regions. But divisions exist also at the level of the single farm, with HYVs being grown in some fields to supply commercial markets and alongside native varieties in others destined for subsistence use.

Even in areas dominated by cultivation of HYVs for the market, some traditional varieties are grown and in this way a high degree of genetic diversity can be retained. This has been found to be the case for potatoes in Peru and maize in Mexico. It appears that small-scale farmers tend to use a mixture of improved and native varieties without making any clear cultural distinction between the two categories. The balance will result from weighing up the advantages of higher yields of the HYVs alongside positive traits of the native varieties. These may taste better or store better than HYVs, for example, and frequently are associated with lower risks than the newer technologies.

Most small-scale farmers are long accustomed to cultivating several fields and to mixing crops and technologies within a single field. The choice of which varieties to grow, therefore, is not an all or nothing one. Farmers will experiment with new crops and technologies; for example, native crops may be cultivated with modern technology, such as chemical pesticides, and introduced varieties may be grown using indigenous tools and cultivation methods. Because of this, it would appear that the elimination of all native varieties is a rare phenomenon among indigenous peasant farmers, not so much a result of resistance to change as a means of keeping options open for meeting different goals and needs in heterogeneous environments. Some farmers' groups, for example, are focusing their efforts on growing their own seeds without making clear distinctions between local varieties and imported ones.

There are three main types of grassroots genetic conservation efforts in Latin America:

○ Small farmers all over the continent continue to grow native varieties as integral parts of their farming systems, and some are now giving a renewed emphasis to traditional systems as they can no longer afford the costs of Green Revolution technology.

○ Various types of development NGO are working, usually with farmers, to conserve genetic resources.

○ Scientists from public research institutes, increasingly aware of the need and urgency of *in situ* conservation, are initiating some efforts in this area. They make a clear distinction between *in situ* conservation and what is only local seed production; however, projects which are meant to involve the use of collected resources are invariably underfunded.

Presently, most conservation efforts are directed to the three major crops: maize, beans and potatoes. While conservation projects all over Latin America include maize, and the Mexican-based International Centre for the Improvement of Wheat and Maize (CIMMYT) does major work on the crop, it is the Brazilian NGO Projecto Tecnologias Alternativas (PTA) which is leading efforts to link conservation and breeding at the farmer level. NGOs are increasingly involved in potato conservation too, because the efforts of the formal sector do not meet their requirements.

Conservation efforts in tomatoes, *Capsicum* (peppers) and cucurbits (squashes) are far behind those of the three main crops, especially among the NGOs. One reason is that they are not considered to be nutritious basic food crops. Very early introduction of improved varieties and the consequent genetic erosion might also explain the lack of attention given to tomatoes. Quinoa, amaranth and lupin, on the other hand, are three crops which have received growing attention during the last decade. High nutritious value, hardiness, few pests and good yields under marginal conditions are all factors which have triggered this interest. However, the need for rather complex processing, and changing nutritional habits amongst rural and urban populations seem to limit their general use.

The work of the NGOs

A growing number of development NGOs, especially but not exclusively those which work on sustainable agriculture and rural development, has learned from their field experience that autonomous seed production and conservation of local crop varieties are critical factors in any grassroots development strategy. Certain NGOs, like some of the farmers' groups they work with, focus on crops or varieties considered important from a development perspective, and do not necessarily consider their genetic base or whether they are indigenous or native in origin.

Three main strategies are employed for genetic resources conservation: those concentrating on local seed production and distribution; those with an emphasis on plant breeding; and those which promote diversity more directly through farmers' fairs.

Local seed production
Projects in this group involve the collection, reproduction and local distribution of crop varieties which are important or interesting from the point of view of local farmers, whether for commercial, nutritional, subsistence, cultural or agronomic reasons. When it is considered useful, introduced material may be used as well as native varieties. Not all varieties are reproduced, just those demanded by farmers; as collection goes on, however, the tendency is to retain in small seed banks some of the varieties not being used in the fields.

As a variant of this first strategy, some projects focus exclusively on native species. Such projects are more likely to be initiated by NGOs, rather than by farmers' groups themselves; for example the work of CET in *in situ* conservation of native potato varieties in the Chiloe Islands. The archipelago of Chiloe, a group of islands off the coast of southern Chile, is considered to be one of the centres of origin of the potato. One hundred and forty-six native varieties were described in one collecting mission, all highly adapted to the range of regional ecological conditions and of key importance for subsistence production.[5] Since the early 1940s, successive Chilean governments have introduced varieties from Europe and North America, some of which have been bred from Chilotan materials. In areas close to urban and market centres, farmers have abandoned most native varieties in favour of those, such as 'Desirée', 'Industrie', 'Condor' and 'Ginecke', which have greater commercial demand. Diseases have been brought in alongside the introduced varieties. Around 1950, potato blight devastated fields of native varieties which lacked the genetic tolerance to this new pathogen.

In an effort to halt genetic erosion and recover some of the native potato varieties, CET initiated an *in situ* conservation project at its training centre near Chonchi and in several neighbouring rural communities. In 1988, CET technicians had surveyed several agricultural areas of Chiloe and collected hundreds of native samples still grown by small farmers throughout the largest island. The following year, CET established a live collection – a garden genebank – of 96 native varieties; these are maintained and improved every year by continuous selection and enhancement.

In 1990, the *in situ* programme began, with 21 farmers in five different rural communities drawing upon the seed bank of native varieties. Each farmer is given a sample of five native varieties which (s)he grows within her/his potato fields. After harvest, farmers return part of the seed production to CET's garden genebank, exchange seeds with other farmers and also plant them again for further production. It is expected that more farmers will join the project, and that CET will contribute to the selection of varieties, based on farmers' needs and desirable characteristics. Excess seed can be sold to other farmers or exchanged for traditional varieties otherwise not available in CET's collection. Varietal selection and interchange within and between the groups of farmers results in a dynamic system which will allow a continuous supply of seeds to resource-poor farmers for subsistence agriculture, and act as a repository of vital genetic diversity for future regional crop improvement programmes.

Plant breeding

Such projects usually focus on the three big crops, that is, maize, potatoes and beans. Breeding is done mainly through mass selection, although some groups employ crossing techniques. This latter strategy is characteristic of NGOs which often work in collaboration with scientists or governmental agencies. The PTA, for example, has been working this way in Brazil since 1986.

The two strategies require technical support in addition to the input of the farmers themselves and therefore give scientists and development workers the possibility of exerting a strong influence over decisions made and strategies followed. Socially and culturally sensitive professionals are required for these approaches to ensure that the actual needs of farmers are addressed.

Projects to promote diversity

Diversity of crop varieties can be encouraged more directly by a third type of project which leaves most decisions to farmers themselves and requires few financial resources and few facilities. At local farmers' fairs, organized by NGOs or professionals from universities and other public institutes, awards are given to the farmer who keeps the widest diversity and knows best the characteristics of the varieties she or he has saved. The strategy may or may not promote reproduction of exhibited materials; its basic aim is to stimulate farmers to keep diversity in their fields hoping that incentives such as public recognition, diplomas, or tools for the farm will make other farmers adopt or recover local varieties. Like all incentive-based schemes, its effectiveness may vary significantly, but fairs have been organized successfully in Peru and Bolivia, and a growing number of NGOs is now actively promoting the strategy.

The potential for improving local crops

As a major crop genetic centre, Latin America has provided and still offers useful genetic material for the improvement of many crops throughout the world. For example, the Mexican *Solanum demissum* has provided genes for resistance to late blight, bacterial wilt, several viruses and nematodes as well as frost tolerance to commercial potato varieties; several native varieties from the Andean region have likewise provided useful genetic characteristics. A wild perennial barley from Chile, *Hordeum chilense*, has had considerable value in wheat breeding programmes. There are numerous examples. In essence, the genetic diversity maintained in traditional Latin American agro-ecosystems has been crucial to the survival and stability of modern agriculture in industrialized countries.

Genes found in native crops can also provide resources to support a more sustainable agriculture directed at the needs and constraints of local peasant farming. Little research, however, has been conducted on exploring the genetic potential of wild relatives and landraces of direct value to local communities, but some beginnings have been made to conserve species which were previously ignored. The International Agricultural Research Centres (IARC) in the region have expanded their conservation efforts for quinoa, yam, ulloco and oca, and several universities and national research institutes are showing renewed interest in these areas. In general, though, while there is an increased awareness of the importance and urgency to conserve these crops, adaptive research on local varieties, which would provide tolerance to drought or other environmental extremes, better productivity under marginal regimes or improved nutritional quality, is still very limited.

Tarwi (*Lupinus mutablis*), for example, is an important crop which not only has higher oil and protein content than newer, introduced legumes, but is also more resistant to environmental stresses and often planted as an insurance crop in mixtures with maize or broad beans. It is also a hardy green manure crop with excellent potential for fitting into crop rotation schemes; yet no formal breeding efforts have been made to boost yields or to select for early maturing varieties.

Similarly, Mashua (*Tropaeolum tuberosum*) is a high-yielding cold resistant crop. It repels many insects, nematodes and pathogens, making it a valuable plant to intercrop with oca, ulluco and potatoes. Yet no serious evaluation of its potential has been made. Over 50 Andean crops with high agronomic potential are in danger of becoming extinct without the necessary crop improvements to adapt them to current farming practices. These include various species of potato with frost hardiness, heat tolerance or other characteristics, several grains and legumes which grow well in mixtures, as well as over 20 species of fruits and nuts. This is a clear example of where redirected research priorities could enhance conservation efforts by improving the productivity of minor crops.

Impact and efficiency of genetic conservation efforts

It is difficult to evaluate how significant these initiatives have been to genetic conservation in Latin America. What is meant by 'genetic conservation' or 'genetic erosion' is often not clearly defined, particularly not from the farmers' point of view. If we were to measure genetic diversity, how would we value one variety against another? Does erosion mean loss of genes or loss of varieties?

One point is certain, though. Genetic conservation at the grassroots level aims to cover needs which big, centralized national or international genebanks do not. Grassroots efforts have been set up *because* the formal sector is not meeting the needs of the small peasant farmers. It is clear that there will be an increasing demand for this type of work, which means that it will become increasingly important to address thoroughly some of the technical questions and limitations of grassroots approaches, like those we are experiencing in Latin America.

11 Promoting local conservation in Ecuador

MIGES BAUMANN*

Genetic diversity, and the traditional technologies and cropping systems which farmers have used to develop and utilize it, is the logical long-term basis for sustainable agriculture. Against the power of government propaganda and the narrow interests of the agrochemical sector, Swissaid is trying to promote a more ecologically sound and socially balanced approach within its agricultural development projects to empower farmers to recover and develop their own capacities in resource management. This approach to its project work is backed up by awareness-raising and policy work at home.

Professor Guillermo Albornoz is regarded in Ecuador as the 'grandfather of the potato'. At Quito University, and later at the National Institute for Agricultural Research (INIAP), he studied and bred new varieties of potato. However, the aged professor reacts with embarrassment to this honorary title, saying that there are many other, more important 'grandfathers and grandmothers', meaning the Andean farmers who have been selecting a wide diversity of *Solanum* tubers for millennia, even before the time of the Incas. They are the ones who have produced thousands of different potato varieties which were very well adapted to local ecological systems and nutritional requirements. Professor Albornoz takes a rather critical view of his own work and considers that some of the new potato varieties developed by the INIAP were not tested long enough and were released too early, with the result that they showed little resistance to disease when planted by farmers.

* Miges Baumann has been focusing on issues related to genetic resources, biotechnology and Third World agriculture for nearly ten years, particularly as a journalist. He currently works for the Swiss development agency Swissaid, where he is responsible both for helping the organization strengthen its project work on genetic resources and raise awareness within the general public about the importance of local conservation for sustainable development.

116

The new varieties bred by the Institute, for example Gabriela, Santa Cecilia, Esperanza or Santa Maria, are recommended and propagated by INIAP and government agricultural advisors. Anibal and Orfelina Correo, who live in the remote hamlet of Boliche in Simiatug, have their own story to tell about this:

> The agronomists came and encouraged us to set up a co-operative. They brought us new varieties of potatoes and artificial fertilizer and started field tests. Initially, the new seed potatoes gave a much higher yield with different fertilizers. And we believed that what came from the Whites was better than what we had had in the past. But then the yield began to fall the very next year. In the third year, they were plagued by worms. The agronomists brought in fungicides and pesticides to deal with the pests, but the chemicals got more expensive every year. We also had to increase the pesticide dose all the time. The potatoes began to taste bitter because we were spraying so much.

Artificial fertilizer is very expensive. 'Six years ago, we could buy a sack of artificial fertilizer for a sack of potatoes. Today, the same sack of fertilizer costs six sacks of potatoes,' explains another farmer. Pesticides and new seed potatoes are expensive as well. Disillusioned, Anibal and Orfelina Correo went back to their traditional method of cultivation which had maintained stability in Indian agriculture for centuries, that is back to organic manure, to skilful rotation of crops leaving the ground fallow, and above all to the traditional potato varieties. They were lucky to be able to find them, because in many cases the traditional varieties are lost when modern technology permeates the village and the INIAP potatoes begin to drive out the native ones.

Farmer Belisario also grows potatoes. But in his field near Atapulo, on a 3,700-metre high plateau, he does not plant the varieties advocated by agronomists and the government, nor does he stick to monoculture with one type of potato, as the propaganda intended for 'modern' farmers recommends. Belisario does not need all the pesticides advertised on the radio from 5 a.m. onwards, nor the artificial fertilizers recommended by the potato adviser. He is not a modern farmer, but plants his potatoes the way his ancestors did. He is familiar with every inch of his fields, identifying each variety. He has more than ten different types of potato. One is more resistant to fungus, another withstands a certain beetle, and a third may be less sensitive to night frosts. Yet another one survives drought well, while the next one tastes particularly good. In this way, Belisario can deal safely with climate and pest problems. 'Previously, I used to plant many more different varieties,' he said. 'Not long ago, I rediscovered the Allco Chaqui variety, which had died out here, but still being grown by a farmer in a neighbouring valley.' Once he has warmed up to the conversation, he stops struggling along in Spanish and continues in Quechua. *Allco chaqui* means *Pie de perro*, dog's paw.

Belisario keeps the Allco Chaqui in a little basket in his small thatched clay-brick house, ready for the next season's sowing. The potato really does look like a dog's paw! We joke that it must be hard to peel, and Belisario explains that there is no need to peel it and that it tastes especially good in soup. Incidentally, like all the other traditional potato varieties, it cooks far more quickly than the new INIAP potatoes, thus requiring less wood, a considerable advantage up on the cold, treeless plateau. According to Belisario, 'In this area, everybody cooks the government's Gabriela potatoes separately, because by the time they are ready, our own potatoes have long boiled to mush.' Asked why he plants the old varieties, he answers, 'They taste much better.' Later he elaborates: 'Our varieties bring a good price on the local market because people know and like these potatoes. In the towns, though, people are only familiar with the new varieties, so Gabriela brings a better price there.' That is why the Atapulo farmers plant two different groups of potatoes. 'We eat the traditional varieties ourselves and sell the new ones in the towns.' The traditional varieties are manured with sheep dung, and thrive on it.

The range of potato varieties has been developed alongside the fight against pests. By careful selection, Andean farmers retained the crop's natural resistance and helped develop new ones. The different varieties keep pests at bay and guarantee the farmers a safe harvest. Mountain farmers in the Andes have even developed a clever cultivation system which makes it possible to keep seed potatoes healthy and free from viruses. A farmer in the Simiatug region explained that potatoes from fields lying at 3,700 metres above sea-level were used for seed purposes. Thanks to a traditional system of exchange within the extended family, the healthy seed potatoes were brought down to the fields 1,000 metres below where pressure from pests is considerably greater.

Nowadays, however, the farmers who use these techniques are few; nor are there many who still plant 20 or more different types of potato. The original range of varieties has virtually disappeared. Even staff at agricultural research institutes throughout the Andean states are shocked by the speed at which varieties are disappearing. Carlos Ochoa, who conducts research on potatoes and is the best-known breeder of new varieties in Peru, has a lot to say:

I remember that nearly 25 years ago I was exploring the North of Peru. At that time, it was still possible to find dozens of interesting primitive potato cultivars, but 20 years later it was more difficult to find such variability. Many of them, like Naranja for instance, are probably extinct. The main reason, I am sorry to say, is the introduction of Renacimiento [Rebirth], one of the varieties that I bred, a long time ago, for this country.

National institutes, government development agencies and sometimes even private aid organizations often play a direct role in destroying this diversity. In their development programmes, they tout the new 'high-yielding' varieties (HYVs) bring them to the farmers or help finance the spread of chemical fertilizers and pesticides. In many cases, particularly active farmers' organizations also contribute to the loss of the traditional varieties.

Take the example of the potato farmers in Mulalillo. After a period of drought, the supply of seed potatoes of most of the farmers had been all but wiped out. The farmers' organizations promised to help out and brought in new seed potato varieties developed by the government. At the same time, they built up a small local seed bank from which the farmers could obtain seed potatoes in future, paying for them with part of their harvest. The efficient administration of the seed potatoes by their own organization prompted the farmers to stop planting traditional varieties. However, the resistance of the new ones was exhausted after just a few years, and the crops became plagued with disease. The farmers then realized how dependent they had become in the meantime. Seed potatoes, artificial fertilizer and pesticides all come from external sources and are very expensive.

In Ecuador, Indian organizations have gained a lot of self-esteem in recent years and are increasingly rejecting cultural colonization by Europe and the United States. Renewed awareness of their own values and cultural independence gave birth to a strong political force. The debate about '500 Years of Conquest in Latin America', celebrated by the Indian organizations as '500 Years of Resistance', encourages this awareness. In this political climate, efforts to retain genetic variety fall on particularly fertile ground. Indian organizations in many places are becoming aware that the original varieties of potato are part of their traditional agriculture and thus part of their cultural heritage which should be protected. And the only way the *campesinos* can establish their independent agriculture, which is tailored to local needs and self-sufficiency, is to have access to their own genetic resources, that is to conserve and utilize the different traditional varieties.

The work of Swissaid

The Swissaid Coordination Office in Ecuador is now trying to encourage this approach and to trigger this awareness among partner organizations and farmers. In the regions of the country where the agency has projects, farmers' organizations join forces with it to find how traditional varieties which are still in existence could be reintroduced, used and possibly improved. The expertise and know-how of farmers such as Belisario or Anibal and Orfelina Correo are much in demand for this very reason.

This description of traditional methods of growing potatoes exemplifies how a private development organization can combat genetic erosion and support the conservation of genetic resources. In line with its project policy, Swissaid supports rural initiatives and development efforts by farmers' co-operatives, grassroots organizations, women's groups, community movements and ethnic minority organizations in certain developing countries. It neither has experts in the field, nor does it support programmes which have been initiated externally and are executed with (costly) foreign experts or development-aid staff. On the other hand, in every project country there is a co-ordination office, usually run by local people. These offices liaise with partner organizations, providing them with advice and organizing their financial support.

Since 1988, in its 'Guidelines for Development Work',

Swissaid has defined sustainable, ecological agriculture and the conservation of genetic diversity as an important principle of its agricultural development policy. As a result, a special Agriculture and Environment Department was set up in 1990 at the agency's Berne headquarters in Switzerland. This department works across the vertical national sectors, integrating sustainable agriculture concerns into all the programmes. The idea is to intensify links between environmental issues and rural development work with this department's support. The department focuses, amongst other issues, on the question of how the erosion of genetic diverstiy can be halted, and has launched a campaign stressing the value and importance of diversity, while at the same time trying to prevent the extension of monopoly patent laws to life forms and to give space for the development of 'farmers' rights'. Project work in developing countries is backed up by information and consciousness-raising in Switzerland, and by political lobbying both in Switzerland and in international organizations.

The project regions

Swissaid does not promote genetic resources conservation projects as such, but incorporates conservation criteria in all its agricultural work, for example, water supply and health projects, and projects to strengthen the role of women. In this way, farmers develop confidence in their traditional varieties as they do in their farming systems. In many cases, those traditional systems have become altered and outside help by project agencies may be required to allow the old system to be re-established or, where appropriate, for changes to be made. For example, many small farmers have sold their animals to buy land, although in many cases the land was originally theirs, leaving their farming systems incomplete. Outside support can provide that little push which enables them to re-establish themselves. It might take the form of animals, for example, to provide traction and manure for fertilizer. The projects funded are all grassroots projects which have a community organization that allows full participation by farmers, and where the level of technology used allows it to be controlled by the farmers themselves, with a minimum of outside technical support.

In connection with project work, the question arose as to

how the conservation and utilization of diversity could be encouraged in practice among Third World partner organizations. It soon became clear that the advisory function of co-ordination offices in project countries could play a crucial role. For this reason, the first step was to ensure that the offices were aware of all the relevant issues. The Agriculture and Environment Department in Bern provides the offices with information, for example about the extension of international patent laws to cover genetic material and the possible consequences of such extension. With the expected monopolization of hereditary features by genetic-engineering companies, it is vital for farmers to be able to retain direct access to and control over their plant resources and thus their independence.

Headquarters' staff who are responsible for specific countries and, occasionally, staff from the Agriculture and Environment Department pay regular visits to the co-ordinators and the partner organizations. They encourage them to consider how genetic diversity can be conserved and used. Economic cost/benefit analyses of the work of small farmers in the Third World are usually quick to testify in favour of mixed cropping, traditional adapted varieties and sustainable production methods. However, the ideology of the modern farmer who uses standardized HYVs is being continually hammered home, and many farmers begin to have doubts about their methods in the face of massive propaganda from the chemical industry. They hesitate to trust in their own experience and to continue with, or return to, mixed cropping and the traditional wide range of varieties.

What is more, in the agricultural colleges of many South American countries the students are often informed only about the input- and capital-intensive methods of modern agriculture, with the result that they never hear anything about traditional cultivation methods in the Andes or about organic farming. That is why agronomists sometimes argue that it is impossible to produce for the market without artificial fertilizer and pesticides. This in turn results in one-sided instruction of small farmers by government agricultural advisors.

The question of which technology is applied is also a social issue. The technology of the *campesinos* (the local small farmers) is traditional and based on the old agro-ecological expertise and knowledge of the farming communities. As the 'technology of the poor', it is often dismissed as backward and inferior. In sharp contrast, the rich farmers and estate owners, who are often descendants from European conquerors, have clearly thrown in their lot with Western agriculture. This technology is considered to be progressive and economically promising. State agricultural workers, as well as many development agencies and NGOs, base themselves largely on this technology in their work with *campesinos*. Rural farming communities which do not follow official government programmes are regarded as totally underdeveloped or even obstructive, and clash with government policy or with the local authorities.

By contrast, Swissaid's work has the general aim of promoting a sustainable, low external-input agriculture as well as reinforcing the negotiating position of village communities towards local authorities and government. For its coordination offices, this often means disseminating alternative, concrete information to counter the propaganda from agro-industry sources and reassuring farmers that their agricultural expertise and traditional cultivation methods are extremely valuable. The *campesinos'* technology can obtain the same productivity as the 'technology of the rich'. Efforts to preserve and make good use of diversity should therefore be seen in the context of this larger agricultural policy framework. After all, it is the traditional cultivation methods of the local farming community which created the genetic diversity and wealth of species and kept them alive till the present day.

Creating awareness at home

A further important element in the Swissaid campaign is information work in Switzerland. The Agriculture and Environment Department tries to compensate for the current lack of information, spreading the word about the value and potential of the agro-ecological expertise of local communities in developing countries, for instance, or providing information about the possible repercussions of biotechnologies on the Third World. It introduces these topics into the national media and publishes articles and material on this subject in conjunction with the Information Department, aimed at the general public.

In addition, it organizes an annual symposium which discusses topical issues in connection with agriculture, environmental and development policy. With a view to the 1992 UN Conference for Environment and Development (UNCED), the special department held a symposium in 1991 on the 'Conservation of Plant Genetic Resources, Diversity and Intellectual Property Rights'. It was directed at experts in the field, decision makers working in agriculture, government, politics, economics and in environmental and development organizations. In the same year it also held a workshop on the same topic entitled 'Conservation and Utilization of Diversity in Development: Experiences from the South'. It was intended mainly for the staff of aid and development agencies and aimed at ensuring that conservation and utilization are given greater consideration in development co-operation.

The whole problem also involves highly political issues such as the extension of patent law to life forms, the concept of 'farmers' rights', as debated at FAO, or the GATT and UNCED negotiations. These themes are being taken up and worked on by the Agriculture and Environment Department. Swissaid, in conjunction with other aid organizations, has built up an effective political lobbying instrument in the form of the joint coalition with the Swiss Lenthen Fund, Bread for All and Helvetas. The agency also supports international campaigning organizations in order to ensure that appropriate information and lobbying work is carried out in UN and other international bodies.

12 Towards a folk revolution

PAT ROY MOONEY*

The formal sector is only starting to open its eyes to the fact that farmers innovate and that local communities do and can contribute to conservation and breeding. If the world is properly to conserve and use genetic resources for both present and future generations, the informal sector of the Third World, that is, the farmers, herbalists, gardeners and pastoralists, must lead us into the next agricultural revolution.

Agricultural research has generally been an informal affair. It has also been mostly an affair led by farmers, and, more often than not, farmers in areas we now describe as the Third World. It took Europeans 4,000 years to join the world's first great agricultural revolution, when they finally picked up on how to sow seeds. Even then, Near Eastern farmers personally had to come and show them how. The Near Easterners also showed Europe the way to the second agricultural revolution. Between the seventh and eleventh centuries, Muslim agriculturalists introduced and adapted a vast cornucopia of new crops and cropping systems that made it possible to quadruple production. Europe moved from sowing a field every second year (the custom since Greco-Roman farmers) to harvesting summer and winter crops, in many areas, every year. Africa conducted its own internal revolution a little later when farmers picked up maize and cassava from itinerant Portuguese adventurers and bred them for diverse conditions throughout the continent.

* Pat Mooney, from Canada, has been one of the world's driving forces in the global campaign to halt genetic erosion and restructure the world's genetic resources system closer to the hands and hearts of Third World farmers. He works with the Rural Advancement Foundation International (RAFI). For the past 15 years, Pat and his colleagues have researched and written major works exposing the biases of institutional conservation and plant breeding against the interests of small farmers. Together with Cary Fowler, Pat was awarded the Right Livelihood Award (the alternative Nobel Prize) in 1985, and for the past three years was a member of the Steering Committee of the Keystone International Dialogue on Plant Genetic Resources.

Farmers, not agricultural colleges, invented the wheeled heavy plough, the mouldboard and the horse collar. They invented three-field cultivation systems, devised irrigation machinery and selected, adapted, bred and, in the remarkable case of maize, created new crops. For 10,000 years, an informal innovation system, perhaps better described as folk innovation, operated in untold thousands of field laboratories with countless thousands of creative research minds struggling to sustain their families and their lands.

When the third agricultural revolution began, with the rediscovery of Mendel's laws at the turn of this century, the genius of the informal innovation system was discarded and discounted. Yet the innovations continue and often surface when either Western goodwill and/or technology fails the poor.

For example, Western aid first brought wheat imports to Nigeria, replacing traditional crops and cutting local markets. Then, during the recession of the early eighties, donor governments cut off the supply. Local farmers and artisans switched back to cassava, developing gori fufi and other products to fill the gap. Disaster was averted. On the other side of Africa, Tanzanian farmers took hold of the country's coffee-growing business and now grow and process most of the coffee themselves using locally invented equipment.

Here and there, institution-based researchers are catching on to the importance of folk innovation. The impact of inventive farmers has been sufficient to encourage the African Academy of Sciences to study the Mende farmers of Sierra Leone. Independent of foreign experts, these farmers conduct field trials, testing new seeds against different soil types and comparing results within their community.

In the Horn of Africa, Bo Bengtssom, director-general of a Swedish international research organization, recalls visiting Ethiopian farmers and finding carefully documented variety performance records inscribed on door posts. In Addis, genebank director Dr Melaku Worede waves his arms in supplication to the Amheric farmers he visits who teach him the distinctions between varieties of teff or sorghum. 'They only need to look,' he says. 'I look and see nothing. They look and sort out the different types.'

A serviceable taxonomy is essential to innovative agriculturalists, be they folk- or institution-based. Researcher Calestous Juma describes the Bukusus people of Kenya's

Bungoma region who developed a plant classification system at least as practical as that of the great Northern collector, Linnaeus. NorAgric Observers from the Agricultural University of Norway call this folk taxonomy, and describe the work of Andean potato farmers with a four-level classification system; farmers know an average of 35 types and as many as 50–70 names have been found in single communities. According to NorAgric, some southeast Asian farm communities have a five-level taxonomy for rice involving 78 varieties in a district.

Stephen Brush at the University of California can testify to the importance of good taxonomy. A single Amazon community near Iquitos in Peru culitvates 168 different species among 21 gardens. Seventy-four species were identified in one garden alone. Researcher Bellon Corrales found farmers in a Chiapas community cultivating five races and a dozen local varieties of maize. Jivaro farmers in one Amazon community grow over 100 varieties of manioc (cassava). In a single valley in the Andes, folk innovators may grow between 70 and 100 distinct potato varieties; a typical household keeps 10–12 varieties.

In general, however, industrialized country agronomists are skittish about folk innovation. American scientists devoted most of a decade, for example, to exploring the merits of sorghum varieties collected in Ethiopia rather than ask local farmers who had described them clearly, with names such as 'Milk in My Mouth' for a high-lysine variety and 'Why Bother With Wheat' for the top-milling sorghum.

Folk innovators work with more than food crops. These days, Dr Mwenda Mbaka is studying the herbal remedies of herds people in Machakos, Kenya and an Indian herbal company has begun a campaign to uncover what is becoming known as ethnoveterinary medicines. From Ames, Iowa, a team of researchers has so far documented more than 80, mostly African, non-industrial animal medicines used by rural peoples. Rashaida pastoralists in the Sudan have analysed more than 30 camel diseases and developed highly sophisticated breeding programmes to circumvent disease problems.

Already, about one-quarter of prescription human medicines are derived from plants. In almost every case, the route to the industrial use of each plant has been through rural innovation. In the present world of AIDS, global climate change, biotechnology and biological warfare, the wider applicability and economic market for botanical and microbial 'home remedies' is enormous. Winning access to the germplasm, however, is not enough. Institutional scientists also need access to the genius that knows the germplasm.

Institute-based agricultural scientists, still predominantly male, may find folk innovators especially hard to locate because many of them, some say most, are women. Plant collecting some years ago, Dr Trygve Berg was chased out of a Sudanese field by irate women. Berg, a gentle Norwegian scholar, thought he was guilty of trespassing, but male villagers explained that women always went into the fields in advance of the harvest to gather interesting seeds for future testing. Women, too, are the heroes for Nigel Smith at the University of Florida. Smith talks about the Kayapo women in the Brazilian Amazon who not only breed new crop varieties but preserve representative samples in hillside 'genebanks'. During the 1984 famine in the southern Sudan, Norwegian Church Aid worker Arne Olav Oyhus encountered Toposa women who risked their own lives in order to hide the seeds for the next year's planting. When six men died doing the same thing at the Vavilov Institute during the Siege of Leningrad, the world acknowledged their heroism with plaques and medals.

Folkseed

Language is blocking the North's full appreciation of folk innovation. In fact, the language used within Northern scientific circles is only a reflection of the often arcane attitudes common toward the South. Third World farmers are 'peasants'; they do not 'breed' new 'varieties', they merely 'select' 'landraces' apparently with about the same benign intent with which bees pollinate alfalfa. Indeed, landrace is at the apex of language etiquette. Northern texts and journals, including some of RAFI's earlier writings, are replete with woefully incompetent references to 'primitive' or even 'stone-age' seeds as though it were technically possible to maintain thousand-year-old seed without genetic alteration.

Institution-derived plant varieties are generally referred to as 'modern', or 'value-added' or 'high-(yield, quality, tech or response; fill in the blank as you wish). Third World farmers are assumed to be universally delighted to surrender their own culturally relevant seeds for these exotic moderns even though many farmers see this as the agricultural equivalent of swapping the Elgin marbles for the Rolling Stones.

A more disciplined analysis now contends that farmers' seeds are actually varieties, exceptionally well-adapted to local environmental and socio-economic conditions. Here and there, scientists are arguing that the South's farmers apply creative genius and genuine breeding strategies to both agricultural crops and other plants having medicinal or industrial uses.

But the stereotype of the farmer as hapless country bumpkin is only part of the reason for demeaning farmer-based experimentation. The Western model of agribusiness research does not entertain competition happily and has nothing to gain from acknowledging the validity of decentralized, on-farm, non-commercial innovation. Then, too, the form of innovation in agricultural communities is often collective or communal rather than individualistic; and the inventions are hardly chrome and circuitry – they don't stand out; they are part of a more holistic approach to socio-environmental problem-solving. More from ignorance than élitism, many scientists in the North consider farmers either too risk-shy or too tradition-bound to be true inventors. History records otherwise.

The theory that the poor can't take risks has been defeated. West Africa's Azande farmers actually increase both the number and the complexity of their crop experiments following poor harvests. Faced with *Striga* weed infestation in their millet, farmers in Niger have sought out advice from other Sahelian communities with longer experience and developed strategies to 'trap' *Striga* by inter-planting sesame. From cassava cultivators in the Dominican Republic to potato growers in the Andes and rice farmers in the Philippines, researchers are now looking for, and finding, genuine inventiveness. To the surprise of some, this inventive activity is not stimulated exclusively by necessity but often seems to spring from intellectual curiosity, a sense of aesthetics, or even a sense of humour.

Neither do farmers hesitate to import exotic material when nothing satisfactory is available locally. While Nepalese government researchers screened modern cultivars in vain for a cold-water tolerant variety, a local farmer, they later learned, had introduced such a variety from India some years before.

129

The variety was already well-established in a region two days walk away. Thailand's Khon Kaen University discovered a highly effective system of upland rice–groundnut rotation, entirely the genius of local farmers. The innovative strategy is now being adopted by farmers in other regions, with university support.

In light of all this, I propose that the term folkseed replace landrace and other more derogatory terms. Our experience makes it abundantly clear that farmers are, among many other skills and talents they possess, genuine plant breeders.

The haystack and the needle

We in RAFI, like other northern NGOs working with Third World partners, were all uncomfortably aware that something called 'traditional knowledge' was under-rated and overlooked. But the dominance of institutional technologies in the 1960s and 1970s was such that even the most adventurous among us found it difficult to see how the old ways' might be incorporated into the new. Those who tried were generally relegated to the occult side of agricultural research along with those that dance around cow horns under full moons.

For some of us, the first inkling that farmers could be entrusted (note the word) with endangered seeds came at the 1981 International Technical Conference on Crop Genetic Resources co-hosted by the UN's Food and Agriculture Organization (FAO), the International Board for Plant Genetic Resources (IBPGR) and the UN Environment Programme (UNEP) in Rome. Scientists like Melaku Worede talked with enormous respect of the competence of farmers and their knowledge of folkseeds. Two years later, we decided to float the idea of 'farmer/curators' in *The Law of the Seed* (Dag Hammarskjold Foundation, Development Dialogue, 1983, pp. 1–2). With some notable exceptions, the notion that Third World farmers could back up conventional genebanks was greeted with general abuse in the germplasm community.

The search for farmer/curators in the early and mid-1980s was a bit like looking for a haystack with a needle. We were surrounded by examples but we were using the wrong tools for discovery. Even so, our travel and research turned up proof after proof, from the Philippines to Zimbabwe to

Brazil, that not only could farmers save seeds but that farmers were already saving seeds, and had been doing so for about 10,000 years. Conventional non-governmental organizations (NGOs) began to see a way to work with traditional technologies, and the move toward farmer/curators gathered momentum.

With some trepidation, RAFI produced its Community Seed Bank Kit directed to NGO agricultural workers. Circulated in English, French, Portuguese and Spanish by the thousands, the kit is more of an embarrassment for what it doesn't say than a benefit for what it does. There is, for example, no reference to community plant breeding or other forms of folk innovation. But, it was a start, and, using it, RAFI ventured into a series of regional workshops for NGOs on community seed conservation. The first was held, appropriately, in Addis Ababa, Ethiopia with our old mentor, Melaku Worede, at the Plant Genetic Resources Centre of Ethiopia (PGRC/E) in May, 1987. The Asian workshop followed in December of that year at Batu Malang, Indonesia. Rene Salazar of Southeast Asia Rural Institute for Community Education (SEARICE) took the lead along with Wahana Lingkungan Hiding Indonesia (WALHI). In September 1988, the final, Latin American workshop was hosted with Camila Montecinos of the Centre for Education and Technology (CET) in Santiago, Chile.

In all, about 230 participants representing almost as many NGOs attended the sessions. Only about a quarter of those involved were engaged directly in seed saving; most of the rest were agricultural workers concerned with sustainable agriculture in general or pesticide issues in particular.

Despite pure innocence and the chaotic cacophony of our wild ideas and idealism, the three sessions proved worthwhile. Barely a year after the Addis Ababa workshop, the comprehensive continental programme it recommended was funded and lurching into motion. In Latin America, CET brought genetic resources into the programme of the Latin American Network CLADES. Perhaps the most ambitious and complex of all seed-saving programmes is under way through SEARICE, working in partnership with many of the original Asian workshop participants.

RAFI's Community Seed Bank Kit included the five principles, or laws, of genetic conservation (Box 12.1). In retrospect, we would have liked to attach 'utilization' to every

Box 12.1: Five laws of genetic conservation

1. Agricultural diversity can only be safeguarded through the use of diverse strategies. No one strategy can hope to preserve and protect what it took so many human cultures, farming systems and environments so long to produce. Different conservation systems can complement each other and provide insurance against the inadequacies or shortcomings of any one method.

2. What agricultural diversity is saved depends on who is consulted; how much is saved depends on how many people are involved. Farmers, gardeners, fishing people, medicine makers, religious leaders, carpenters – all have different interests that foreign scientists could never hope to appreciate fully. All segments of a community need to be involved to ensure the total needs of the community are met. The more involvement, the greater the potential to conserve.

3. Agricultural diversity will not be saved unless it is used; its value is in its use. Only in use can diversity be appreciated enough to be saved; and only in use can it continue to evolve, thus retaining its value.

4. Agricultural diversity cannot be saved without saving the farm community; conversely, the farm community cannot be saved without saving diversity. Diversity, like music or a dialect, is part of the community that produced it. It cannot exist for long without that community and the circumstances that gave rise to it. Saving farmers is a prerequisite of saving diversity; conversely, communities must save their agricultural diversity in order to retain their own options for development and self-reliance. Someone else's seeds imply someone else's needs.

5. The need for diversity is never-ending. Therefore, our efforts to preserve this diversity can never cease. Because extinction is forever, conservation must be forever. No technology can relieve us of our responsibility to preserve agricultural diversity for ourselves and future generations. Thus, we must continue to utilize diverse conservation strategies, involve as many people in the process as possible, see that diversity is actively used, and ensure the survival of the farm community, for as long as we want agricultural diversity to exist.

mention of 'conservation' and I would not push for a sixth law: we could be wrong. In fact, if history is any guide, we probably are wrong; we have tended to underestimate the problem, make mistakes and do too little. Everything in plant genetic resource conservation should be repeated to protect against inevitable technical, mechanical and human shortcomings. This reinforces the need for a diversity of approaches. The same kit offers a comparison of the institutional and formal systems (Box 12.2). Despite the lack of subtlety and nuance, the conclusion that the two strategies could ideally be complementary in general holds true.

Lessons from RAFI's experience

Although each programme is structured differently and each operates with complete independence one from the other, certain common threads have emerged:

○ Community-based plant genetic resource conservation has been firmly attached to folk plant breeding and both are understood to be part of the wider work, variously known as sustainable agriculture or agro-ecological development. In fact, NGOs concentrating solely on seed saving should probably be approached with caution.
○ As I have already confessed, while NGO activity has mushroomed in the last few years, we have more often encountered work-in-progress than we have been the instigators of that work. Outside of the farming community, local NGOs have, however, added genetic resources to their rural repertoire and their competence and campaigns have grown by leaps and bounds.
○ Some common needs have also emerged. Rural workers require some practical training in the methodology of plant collecting, germination testing and grow-out organization. Additional training is needed in community documentation and evaluation. A clear need has emerged for research into community-accessible techniques and materials for storage and for plant breeding. Some of the technical problems facing grassroots workers in plant genetic resource conservation are elaborated by Camila Montecinos in Chapter 13. In general, however, institutional scientists might be surprised to discover that their community counterparts have not remained frozen in the

133

Box 12.2: Safeguarding diversity: complementary strategies

The institutional strategy

Surveys

Develops eco-graphical surveys of large land areas using satellite remote-sensing devices combined with interdisciplinary teams of scientists/explorers sampling a wide range of globally important species within a limited time period.

Collection

Organizes a national/international team of crop-specific specialists to collect in a specified region during a multi-week period.

Storage

Samples are stored at controlled temperature and humidity with the aid of highly-trained personnel and state-of-the-art monitoring devices able to maintain the viability of the collection for years or decades without rejuvenation.

Rejuvenation

Optimally, as germination rates decline, a sample is 'grown-out' and the harvested seed is returned to the genebank.

Documentation

Plant Collector's field book is stored and/or computerized. Subsequent information on sample is also computerized and related to other collection data and maps.

Evaluation

Trained scientists using modern laboratory equipment undertake a series of wide-ranging tests to determine the characteristics and potential uses of each sample.

Utilization

Evaluation data are shared with the scientific community and duplicate samples are made available to public and private institutes for possible incorporation into breeding programmes.

pre-Mendelian world of 1900 but have either already employed or are eager to employ any and all recent breeding techniques, including cloning and tissue culture work.

All this bespeaks some generic infrastructural require-

The community strategy

Surveys

Supports socio-ecological surveys of the community land area based upon consultations with farmers, food preparers, medicine makers, gatherers, herders, fisher-folk and artisans involving teams of plant-users in continuous survey and monitoring exercises covering locally important species.

Collection

Organizes a series of community-based collection expeditions covering a large range of crops throughout the entire growing season.

Storage

Cultivars are kept as part of the farming system or, where possible, in small plots for endangered cultivars and/or seed samples are cleaned, dried, and stored under cool/dry conditions within the community and monitored by local people knowledgeable about the species.

Rejuvenation

With a decline in viability, a sample is either grown-out or (if possible) a new sample is collected from the original site.

Documentation

Field collection sheets are copied and filed. Information is kept in most useful local language using locally understood land descriptions for the benefit of further investigation.

Evaluation

Plant collectors discuss characteristics of each sample with the local user at the time of collection. Immediate usefulness and long-term value are documented.

Utilization

Evaluation information is shared with community users and samples may be adopted directly or adapted by community members to improve production.

---

ments that span all continents. Local NGOs need to exchange experiences within a region. Although more and more Southern scientists in the institutional sector are expressing a willingness to work with community groups, great gaps in human resources have emerged everywhere. Often, the only practical advice available for a specific crop or a specific eco-geographical zone is available solely from other community groups. Scientific exchanges between folk innovators are important and augment more traditional training workshops. Regional newsletters, annual or semi-annual training workshops and policy seminars are all needed. Farmers tend to have a healthy, holistic view of their situation and want to look beyond the necessary practical information to the socio-economic context. From seed saving to plant breeding, farm communities move onward to look at quality control, markets and more equal and co-operative relations with their institutional counterparts both nationally and regionally.

This all goes to demonstrate that plant genetic material, to be a truly useful resource, must include a good deal more than the material itself. It must include information about where the genetic material can be found in nature and how it can be used; and access to technologies which make fullest possible use of the resource is required, including both the discrete microtechnologies most commonly created by folk innovators as well as the more generic macrotechnologies generally developed by institutional innovators. All of this must fit in with the farming, marketing and environmental systems within which plant genetic resources operate. Funds are also needed both for the conservation and the utilization of genetic material, otherwise it cannot be considered a resource. We summarize these needs as GIFTS: Germplasm, Information, Funds, Technology and Systems, all five of which must be borne in mind.

Towards a folk revolution in conservation and plant breeding

It may be time for the farmers of the Third World to lead another and very different kind of agricultural revolution. We propose an integrated global campaign to collect, store and use plant genetic resources. At no time in human history has it been more possible to draw in so many minds to help each other solve problems. The Chinese powered their agricultural revolution (from the tenth to the fifteenth centuries) with a seven-fold increase in irrigation projects; Arabs powered their revolution with the introduction of new crops; and the Green Revolution was based on fertilizers. The power behind the next revolution must be human minds, those of the informal innovators. The International Agricultural Research Centres (IARCs) should see the restructuring of their system as a means to engage those minds.

For us in RAFI, the experience of the regional seminars and the follow-up fundraising and practical support with each region has forced us to contemplate a possible contradiction: farm communities, as a matter of survival, need to have control over the whole plant genetic resources process; yet, the world community, also as a matter of survival, needs the same plant genetic resources in order to achieve some semblance of global food security. Co-operation between the formal and farmer-based innovation and conservation systems is therefore vital.

This amounts to not so modest a proposal. It would demand that agricultural research be restructured, reintroducing farmers as full and active partners in innovation. Their genius, their knowledge, their field laboratories and their very diversity are essential forces in creating a people-based agricultural revolution that will allow the poor to eat and the earth to survive. Farmers could benefit from such a redirection of research priorities. But equally, for the institutional system to overlook and ignore the tremendous opportunity that folk innovators offer would amount to criminal negligence. The agricultural revolution to come will not depend upon macrotechnical changes but the application of microtechnical improvements in a million places, aided by computers, biotechnology and collective genius working in a just socio-economic environment.

Farmers could play a major role, in fact *the* major role, in the collection of genetic material. A massive global plant genetic resource exercise is required and RAFI's calculations show that the feasibility of such an exercise could be increased by community involvement while the cost would be vastly reduced. Collection costs from now until the end of the century, for example, could be cut from US$84 million to US$28 million, and the total costs of the conservation campaign cut by over US$1000 million (see Annex 12.1).

But farmers must also play the major role in plant breeding. (Annex 12.2 outlines a possible apporoach.) We have had to revise our earlier view of 'farmer/curators'. Farmers, as we have been arguing, are not museum curators but genuine innovators. Like formal-sector scientists, they are breeders who conserve genetic diversity because they know they need it. Ten years ago we fought at FAO and with

IBPGR over the right and competence of farm communities to conserve genetic diversity in partnership with genebanks. Now the debate is to establish the right and competence of farmers to continue plant breeding, and to work in partnership with formal-sector colleagues in this task. Ten years ago, genebank directors, with rare exceptions, wondered why farmers needed to save their own seeds, why they couldn't simply rely upon genebanks to take care of their needs. Today, many scientists in international agricultural research centres cannot understand why farm communities don't leave the breeding to the formal sector. Brazilian farmers answered the questions best in 1989 at the Santiago workshop: poor farmers can't trust rich scientists. The poor can never trust the rich to understand, act on, or continue to support the interests of poor people. Our fourth law in community seed banking mentions 'Someone else's seeds imply someone else's needs'; of itself, this could become the first law of community plant breeding.

Discussions must begin with the international agricultural research centres and the UN agencies, as well as with national governments, on ways and means to support folk innovations in agriculture and to link those innovations with a more responsive institutional research network. The institutional sector needs to understand that co-operation with folk innovators amounts to no rejection of high technology; it is, in fact, an opportunity to adapt at least some of the rather flexible and inexpensive information processing and safe forms of biotechnology for local use. This does not change, however, what is a sad and fundamental truth: any new technology introduced into a society which is not just will inevitably exacerbate the differences between rich and poor. The political control and social context for any new technique, introduced from the village or from the corporation, must be examined closely. But no new technology should be rejected before it is studied. Many aspects of biotechnology can be used in rural communities under local conditions and control. Folk innovators, after all, genetically engineered maize.

The final lesson in our experience remains that of diversity. The need for local solutions to local conditions is paramount, which means local control over plant genetic resources. This, in turn, requires clear contractual understandings between institute-based and community-based innovators when the two try to work together.

Annex 12.1: The Global Conservation Campaign

A massive global plant genetic resource collection exercise is required. The Keystone International Dialogue Series on Plant Genetic Resources, at its final plenary session, recommended that the eight-year period from 1993 to 2000 should see an intensive campaign at all levels to secure the first link in the world's food chain, that is, the seeds. Genebank authorities estimate that the collection work for major crops is only about half done and they concede that some material in banks now needs to be recollected because of sample sizes or germination problems. Collecting work in 'poor people's crops', which tend to be more locally or regionally important, has barely begun. Farmers should play a full part in such an integrated global campaign to collect, store and use plant genetic resources. After years of both practical and political activity on the international stage, the time has come for serious discussions with the institutional conservation system, especially with FAO and the International Plant Genetic Resources Institute (formerly IBPGR) and the directors of national and IARC genebanks. This discussion need not be polemical but practical. By RAFI's reckoning, the active participation of farm communities in plant genetic resources conservation would not only improve the quality of conservation work but save the world a lot of money as well.

The global collection campaign

Internationally, the average cost of collecting a single sample is estimated at US$40; we estimate that this cost will rise to at least US$56 for conventional crops by the end of the century. For less common species and for specialty collection missions, costs will probably soar to well above US$400 a sample. The institutional sector is handicapped with time limitations and a lack of familiarity with local folk varieties.

By contrast, the community sector can collect throughout the entire harvest period and can much more readily identify unique samples of local crops. It also knows what is endangered and what is not. Farm communities supported by local NGOs can do a much more efficient and much cheaper job. The average cost of collecting a single sample ranges from a high of US$10 in Latin America to a low of US$3 in some parts of Asia and Africa.

Were the institutional system to undertake a global collection campaign to double current collections by the year 2000 (a technically plausible and necessary goal) without community help, the cost for 1.75 million new samples would be nothing less than US$84 million. With NGO/community campaigns taking on 75 per cent of the collection work, at an estimated cost of US$7 million, the total co-ordinated campaign would drop to US$28 million, a saving to the world community of at least US$56 million.

The struggle for storage

Doubling the number of unique accessions will also pose a massive demand for the construction of new genebanks and additional facilities in existing banks. Then, too, new accessions must be duplicated in one or more locations and old collections inadequately stored must be found safer havens and also duplicated. We have estimated that less than a third of present-day collections are in long-term storage and duplicated. Conservatively, more than six million accessions will need new accommodation.

On its own, the institutional system would build new facilities at an average cost of US$75 per sample, rising to more than US$92 each by the year 2000, for a total one-time charge of more than US$512 million. Farm communities could provide *circa situ* (as distinct from *in situ* or *ex situ*) field plots and short-term storage facilities at an average cost of US$2.50 per accession. An entire duplicate set of the world collection could be kept with the farmers who created it for a construction cost of about US$35 million. The global bill for construction would be almost halved to US$291 million, a saving of US$221 million.

Maintenance and evaluation

Once collected and stored, more than seven million seed samples still require to be maintained and evaluated. If extinction is forever then so is conservation. At an estimated annual cost per accession of US$50 (up to US$61 by 2000), the institutional circle would pay out well over US$1.9 billion to the end of the decade and more than US$437 million every year thereafter.

With farm communities taking over one set of duplicate samples at an average cost of US$5 per accession per year, maintenance costs to the end of the global campaign would plummet by almost one billion dollars. The community cost? Twenty-one million. Annual maintenance costs for communities would run to less than US$15 million, allowing the institutional folk to reduce the total annual conservation budget to a much more bearable US$266 million. The long-term annual contribution of farm communities, then, would show up in a yearly saving of more than US$171 million.

Circa situ maintenance and evaluation makes enormous scientific sense as well. Rejuvenation can take place in the same soil and conditions, allowing for much more reliable gene conservation. Farmers can make a tremendous substantive contribution to evaluation and documentation; the collection will be a living, evolving genebank rather than one frozen forever in time.

Infrastructure and development

Apart from basic collection, construction and maintenance costs, the Keystone Dialogue also proposes hefty budgets for research, public education, training and co-ordination. Here, co-operation with rural societies means additional costs. Our crude estimation is that these costs would not exceed US$90 million through to the year 2000 and would probably then level off at US$15 million a year. In sum, and based upon the seed accession estimates made in the Keystone Dialogue, we conclude that the close co-operation with farm communities and local NGOs would slash the costs of the 1993 to 2000 campaign by more than US$1.3 billion.

Annex 12.2: Towards an integrated plant breeding system*

'Informal' plant breeding by farmers and 'formal' breeding by professionals in companies and research institutes are two different systems, in most cases acting in almost complete

---

* This annex is based upon the NorAgric study *Technology Options and the Gene Struggle* by Tygrave Berg, Asmund Bjornstad, Cary Fowler and Tore Skroppa, 1991. For full details refer to the bibliography.

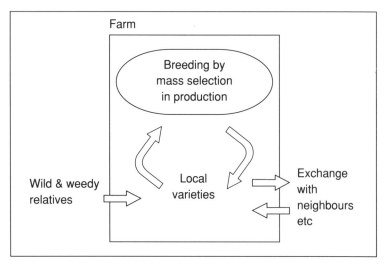

(a) *Plant breeding by the informal, farm sector.*

Figure 7.   *Plant breeding in the formal and informal systems are almost completely separate at present. In the informal, farm, system (a) plant breeding is integrated with production and is carried out continuously by farmers as they select from each harvest. In the formal system (b) plant breeding is carried out by professional plant breeders, separate from farm production. Although farmers' local varieties (and wild and weedy relatives) are the ultimate source of most genetic material, the two systems are not integrated. Instead the genetic resource base of local varieties is eroded by displacement by uniform, improved varieties and by 'modern' agricultural methods.*

142

isolation from each other (Figure 7a & b). But the two systems could be brought together, drawing upon the comparative advantages of each (Figure 8).

In such an integrated breeding system, professional plant breeders would perform the germplasm enhancement part of the breeding basically in the same way as in conventional breeding. The final selection and variety testing, however, would be taken over by farmers.

The integrated system would have a number of advantages:

○ It would produce a large number of heterogeneous varieties adapted to local conditions rather than the few formal system. And while the formal system produces stable varieties, the integrated system would produce varieties which continued to evolve.

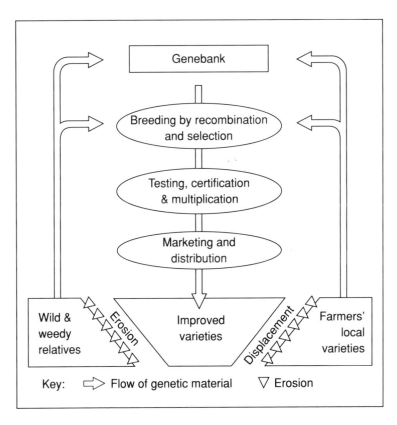

(b) *Plant breeding by the formal sector with erosion of genetic resource base by displacement.*

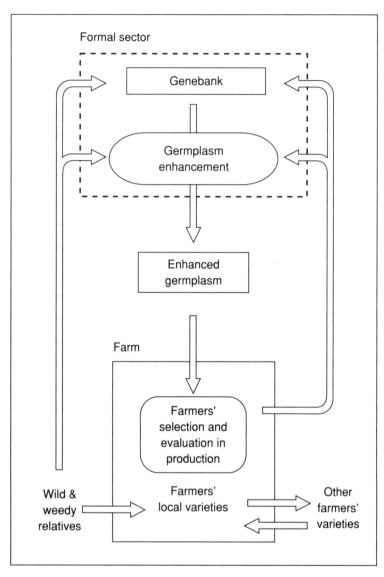

Figure 8. *In an integrated system of plant breeding, the formal sector would produce enhanced genetic material using advanced techniques and drawing upon a worldwide collection of genetic resources. Final selection and evaluation of locally adapted varieties would be carried out by farmers, integrated with production. There would also be an important two-way exchange of information between plant breeding stations and local communities.*

144

○ It would be quicker. Presently the formal system needs 10 to 20 years from initiation of a breeding programme until the result is available to the farmer. Some of this time is used for the breeding itself, some for achieving uniformity and some for testing. The integrated system would short-circuit these phases and varieties would soon become widely available through farmer-to-farmer exchange mechanisms.

○ Over-dependence on genebanks would be reduced and the genetic resource base would be kept in the custody of millions of farmers. Control over genetic resources would be at farmer level.

The integrated system would not guarantee that particular landraces are conserved; it would, however, ensure that a wide range of genetic diversity was maintained, and continued to evolve, on-farm.

The proposal for an integrated system of plant breeding is not as radical as it sounds. With animal breeding, such a participatory approach has proved to be not only feasible but superior to more formal systems. Breeding is in the hands of the farmer, while modern tools such as artificial insemination and computerized recording of animal performance are used. Up until 1930 the USA promoted farm-level crop diversity by sending millions of samples of untested seeds to farmers who performed on-farm research and selection to produce a huge number of crop varieties. The US experiment with grassroots breeding eventually fell victim to a political desire to privatize the seed industry. In most developing countries such a choice has not been made and it is still possible to include traditional breeding in development strategies.

13   Facing the challenge of grassroots conservation

CAMILA MONTECINOS*

While the economic and political barriers to a greater role for farmer-based conservation strategies are great, the methodological and technological problems of grassroots conservation itself cannot be ignored. What should we conserve, breed or use? And how? Answers to these questions must be found to allow farmers and community-based non-governmental organizations (NGOs) to realize their potential in the conservation of genetic resources.

After so many years of controversy and debate, it looks like a common, and common-sense, view is finally starting to emerge. *In situ* conservation strategies, rooted in local communities and developed over centuries by small farmers all over the world, are a necessary and vital complement to large national or international genebank programmes. Although some fundamental political and economic questions are yet to be resolved, it seems that this parallel approach is already acceptable, and that once political consensus is reached, it will just be a matter of getting down to work.

However, a global political consensus on the control and management of plant genetic resources will probably not be reached for many years to come. In the meantime, concrete support to genetic conservation by farmers will probably remain as scattered and insufficient as it is today. Both aspects will dominate discussion on genetic resource conservation for the next few years and will certainly consume the attention and energy of those working for the survival of farmers and genetic diversity. And their urgency and critical importance will probably overshadow yet another fundamental

---

* Camila Montecinos is a Chilean agronomist. She works with the Centro de Educación y Tecnología (CET), an NGO which carries out research and provides technical training on sustainable agriculture and energy to farmers and their organizations throughout the southern half of Chile. Camila is responsible for CET's work in the field of genetic resources.

problem: developing workable, appropriate *in situ* conservation and breeding techniques. The experiences laid out in this book illustrate a very wide range of NGO approaches to *in situ* conservation. It is now assumed by many that we have an ensemble of satisfactory techniques to conserve and make use of genetic diversity, and that we even have a new set of tools, namely biotechnology, which will solve every other problem traditional technologies still come across. Unfortunately, this technological optimism does not correspond to reality. The pace of genetic erosion is still dramatic, and we would be committing a serious mistake in laying the blame on political and economic factors alone.

The technological and methodological problems haunting plant genetic conservation and enhancement at the community level must not be underestimated. Not only do they exacerbate negative pressures, such as the lack of resources, but they are often the underlying cause of many inefficient or aborted efforts. It is important to understand that these technical deficiencies which we come up against reflect not only limitations in human capacities and willpower, but also limitations due to the environment. A widespread problem faced by *in situ* conservation and improvement programmes is that they operate within deteriorating environments which are little understood. Centuries of erosion of human cultures has led to the loss of much age-old knowledge and understanding; and ecological degradation takes with it the availability and value of much accumulated wisdom in environmental management. Reduced genetic diversity means that the full spread of possibilities which were once offered is simply no longer available.

All this would suggest that *in situ* conservation is a science now in great difficulty, one which needs to be salvaged and rebuilt. And in rebuilding and revitalizing it, it is essential to look for its original features. It was a popular science, requiring neither the help of university technicians nor the intervention of experts. It was as deeply rooted in the daily life of peasant farmers throughout the world as the arts of sowing and harvesting. Therefore, the knowledge of the peasant farmer is by matter of course the starting basis of this reconstruction, although various external contributions are equally necessary. In fact, the most difficult aspects of this rebuilding is the necessity of combining the perspective of the peasant farmer with that of conventionally trained technicians, whose education usually provides only partial and superficial grounding in *in situ* conservation.

One critical problem for plant genetic resources conservation and utilization at the community level is the absence of a clear grassroots technical approach. What should we conserve, breed, use or adopt? And how? Although local communities have conserved and bred plant varieties for centuries, cultural erosion and technological and economic pressures have instilled within everyone the belief that local people do not have much to contribute. These forces have also succeeded in divorcing the conservation and promotion of genetic diversity from production, especially commercial production. One way or another, these biases have had a widespread influence among field workers and even farmers, provoking the prejudices and shortcomings characteristic of genetic conservation and utilization at the community level. Some of the most common are discussed here.

Approaches to conservation

Many criteria, methodological decisions or technical options are usually, and sometimes inadvertently, imposed by technical or other non-local workers. This often leads to mistakes with such a range of negative impacts that a whole programme may fail. But whether the criteria or methods prove right or not, this approach itself tends to deny the real and widespread local participation within a strategy of *in situ* conservation and creates dependency instead. A by-product is that many conservation projects end up, usually unwillingly or unintentionally, focusing their work on the good management of small seed banks. Although these banks are normally better adapted to local farmers' needs than national or international genebanks, they still have the deficiencies inherent to any: the inability to store the vast range of plant varieties in use; the halt in evolution; choices based according to technical criteria such as the seed's ability to withstand storage conditions, rather than agricultural relevance; high risk of loss; and the need of an infrastructure which demands a lot of work and funds in order to be well-kept.

It is not easy, nor really the point, simply to avoid imposing our own criteria and enhance farmers' participation instead. The right approach demands a deep social, cultural and economic understanding of the local communities by the external agent(s). It also requires experience, ability, a good methodology and a strong personal commitment to farmers, their needs and demands. But it also calls for a technical understanding of what farmers say and what their contributions are. It is not enough just to note and appreciate what farmers know; it is necessary to understand and respect *how* they use their knowledge, and to look for new ways to widen and enhance its possible uses. This ability cannot be acquired only by a random contact with farmers. It must also be a matter of serious and systematic study.

Many local groups or organizations currently working with seeds, including some farmers' organizations, disregard what the local community has, or assign no role to genetic diversity, paying no attention to the conservation and utilization of local genetic resources. Many local seed programmes, aided or led by well-meant technical extension workers, are concerned merely with autonomous seed production, and have inadvertently become agents of genetic erosion, as they have enhanced the introduction of new, modern commercial varieties. Rural development NGOs are not necessarily an exception to this.

A second characteristic deficiency among technical workers, under this heading, is our poor knowledge of the web of relationships between genetic diversity and the agro-ecosystem as a whole. For instance, there is a strong tendency to forget that the available diversity evolved along with, and thanks to the existence of, a number of different ecosystems where different farmers' options were also a source of diversification, and not under the conditions of monoculture and environmental homogeneity which prevail nowadays. Therefore, it is also usually forgotten that each landrace or traditional variety needs a certain environment or range of environmental conditions to exist as such, and that we therefore need simultaneously to conserve genotypes and adequate environments. Many seed programmes or even plant genetic conservation projects have eliminated or totally neglected the surrounding diversity; nor have they tried to conserve the surrounding agro-ecosystem as a whole. Conversely, many ecosystems are violently altered, and traditional practices, such as polycultures, environmental pest management or microclimatic management, are usually abandoned.

Environmental homogeneity and the aggressive disruption of traditional agro-ecosystems have led to the extinction of many varieties and therefore of on-the-field conservation strategies. This in turn has led many projects to set up seed banks as the only viable strategy, widening the artificial gap between genetic conservation and production. It is necessary to relate genetic to natural resources conservation, and to promote agro-ecological management systems which make possible the conservation, regeneration and new creation of small farmers' cropping systems.

Unfortunately, these needs go against the kind of training technicians usually have. We have learned to specialize and to focus on the crops, usually just a few crops. We need now to learn about production systems, and about crops and their environment, including their relationships to farmers' perceptions and needs. Once again, this is an effort that should be undertaken by different sectors, with farmers playing an important role.

A third kind of deficiency is the lack of appropriate training in genetics and seed management among technicians involved in conservation projects. Appropriate training involves both depth and approach. Training for *in situ* conservation with farmers' participation needs to be clearly set apart from the training required by a plant breeder working for a big seed company. For instance, not knowing the necessary conditions for the conservation of highly adapted landraces may have no effect on the work done by a large company or by a national research institute with a Green Revolution approach. But it has led to the loss of valuable landraces that were conservation targets for local programmes. Another cause for losing landraces has been inadequate environmental control of pests and diseases, especially during storage, something conventional plant breeders can easily control with chemicals.

Plant-breeding techniques and objectives

Breeding techniques and approaches must be different at the community level. So far, there is consensus on the need to work with mass selection, but there are no clear guidelines or principles on, for example, how to select (according to one or several characteristics?), how efficient this approach can be on different species, or how to choose between different

150

needs which cannot be addressed simultaneously (for instance, high yield and resistance). And although mass selection is clearly a basic tool for breeding at the local level, is this the only important tool? It is not so utterly common to meet farmers who have developed their own hybridization techniques. How could the potential of these techniques be assessed or enhanced?

Many other questions in the field of genetics and breeding have so far produced answers which are not necessarily the most appropriate for local genetic conservation work by and for small farmers. For example, should community-based breeders work towards disease and pest resistance, as is traditionally accepted, or should we breed for tolerance to the same problems? If we all know that any kind of resistance creates a pressure barrier which will ultimately be overcome by the appearance of a new type of virulence, would it not be more rational to breed for tolerance, which may allow a much more longer-lasting, non-harmful co-existence? Would it be possible to breed for some sort of ever-evolving resistance? For instance, some sort of mass selection which will rejuvenate resistance after each crop or after a certain number of years, before new sanitary problems arise? Is this not what small farmers have been doing for centuries?

Viruses are another good example of current answers which are not necessarily the best for *in situ* genetic conservation and utilization. We have learned that viruses are accumulative, that the only solution is the periodical cleaning-up of seeds, something which is considered to be extremely difficult to achieve on farmers' fields. In crops plagued by viruses, such as potatoes and beans, seeds need to be renewed periodically, obtained from new, virus-free stocks, and reproduced in isolated or aseptic environments. It is currently accepted that the most efficient, and perhaps the only practical, method to produce new, virus-free stocks is tissue culture. However, Latin American small farmers have grown beans and potatoes for centuries. They are now facing some serious virus problems. But if these problems had existed for as many centuries as the crops do, it would be impossible to produce anything today. Small farmers must have developed some method to keep viruses under control or done some periodical cleaning-up. And they did. Seed production and crop production in different ecological environments and altitudes are just one element of their sophisticated systems we barely know about nowadays. Many questions could still be asked. Did farmers literally clean up their germplasm, or were they able just to maintain some sort of acceptable co-existence between plants and diseases? Did they have any other mechanism to lessen the negative effects of viruses? Could modern science uncover such co-existence mechanisms?

Priorities for conservation

Finally, a series of technical questions which causes deep concern among all involved in genetic conservation has to do with what is genetic erosion/conservation, and what and how much needs to be conserved. There seems to be general consensus that we can not conserve everything, but we need to set some clear priorities and focus on them. The big question is whose priorities. A second one is the timeframe. Should they be long-term or short-term priorities? How can we even decipher long-term needs, especially if the environment is undergoing such profound changes?

Some sectors consider that the new biotechnologies offer the best answers so far. Since biotechnology theoretically enables us to keep 'DNA libraries', we can now focus on keeping genes, not genotypes, thus avoiding duplication and widening our storage capacities. Even if all the technical difficulties associated with DNA libraries could be solved, something which has not yet been done, this approach is completely absurd from the farmers' perspective. Farmers do not use isolated genes, nor can they take genes from a library and blend them at will as a biotechnologist theoretically might. They use varieties or landraces; that is, they use extremely complex and functional genetic populations which took millennia to evolve and select. To take out or insert one or more genes and devise new functional combinations is not an easy task, even for a biotechnologist. It is therefore genotypes which farmers need to conserve.

But clearly no conservation programme could cover all existing genotypes. Similarly, there is no way to predict all future needs. No matter what priorities are set now, they will sooner or later prove wrong or inappropriate for many. The only sound conservation strategy seems to be the one that recognizes as many priorities as possible and provides for the maintenance of as many genotypes as possible.

Different priorities may be set only by different actors, and the highest number of surviving genotypes will be achieved only if the greatest possible environmental diversity is taken into account. Since environmental diversity is the product of the interaction between nature and people, it is dependent on the input of different people. In fact, the history of plant genetic resources teaches us that genetic diversity was created through the participation of countless different uncoordinated rural communities all over the world. If we are to keep, use and regenerate diversity, then we need a strategy that in the long run tends once again to make *in situ* genetic conservation as familiar to every small farmer as sowing or harvesting is now. This way, *in situ* genetic conservation could be enhanced by, but would not depend upon, conservation programmes *per se*, the same way the existence of agriculture does not depend upon the existence of extension programmes.

Clearly, such a strategy will not be easy to carry through. It needs the promotion of a different kind of agriculture; it demands a wider and stronger role played by farmers; it would depend on technicians who understand that *in situ* genetic conservation needs a real, massive and totally free participation of farmers, that is, participation according to their own options and criteria; and it also needs new technical approaches and answers to promote, support or regenerate farmers' skills.

New technical and methodological approaches do not start out from zero. It is necessary to use all the knowledge which already exists. We need therefore to create opportunities to deal with these questions, share the already existing answers and create new ones where necessary. Systematic studies are needed, and the role of universities and research institutes is critical. Bur farmers' knowledge is fundamental. We should be careful to avoid the mistake of once again leaving farmers out of our own learning process.

NGOs can play a crucial role in linking farmers and scientists, as they are the ones who can most likely promote farmers' participation in plant genetic conservation. But most NGOs, even those already working with genetic resources, cannot do that with the human and financial resources they currently have at their disposal. The solutions or answers to the problems we have discussed here need, among other things, the allocation of new resources for training and maintaining at least a minimal corps of well-prepared field workers. Most grassroots genetic conservation programmes are alive thanks only to the strong will and commitment of those involved, who work with very little or no funding and absolutely no time to study or seek out important information. NGOs may be making numerous and important mistakes, but they are doing the best they can with the resources they have. If people already involved with the conservation and utilization of plant genetic resources at the community level had the resources and opportunities for getting more appropriate training as well as for doing more field research, their work would doubtless improve tremendously, and their contribution to an authentic *in situ* conservation and utilization could be priceless.

Annexes

Acronyms used in this book

(Countries in parentheses represent headquarters or country of location)

ASEAN   Association of Southeast Asian Nations
BIMAS   Mass Guidance Programme (Indonesia)
BINHI   A Filipino NGO
CET   Centro de Educación y Tecnología (Chile)
CGIAR   Consultative Group on International Agricultural Research (Washington, Rome)
CIMMYT   Centro Internacional de Mejoramiento de Maís y Trigo (Mexico)
CIP   Centro Internacional de la Papa (Lima, CGIAR)
CLADES   Consorsio Latinoamericano para la Agroecología y Desarrollo (Chile)
DNA   Deoxyribonucleic acid
ENDA   Environment and Development Action (Zimbabwe)
FAO   UN Food and Agricultural Organisation (Rome)
GATT   General Agreement on Tariffs and Trade (Geneva)
GPSN   Gabinete de Produçao de Sementes do Niassa (Mozambique)
GRAIN   Genetic Resources Action International (Spain)
HYV   High-yielding variety
IARCs   International Agricultural Research Centres (CGIAR)
IBPGR   International Board for Plant Genetic Resources (Rome, CGIAR)
ICRISAT   International Crops Research Institute for the Semi-Arid Tropics (Hyderabad, CGIAR)
INIAP   Instituto Nacional de Investigación Agropecuaria (Ecuador)
INMAS   Intensive version of BIMAS (above)
INSUS   Intensive Technology Package (Indonesia)
IRRI   International Rice Research Institute (Los Baños, CGIAR)
KENGO   Kenya Environment and Energy Organizations
MASIPAG   Farmer–Scientist Partnership for Development (Philippines)
NGO   Non-governmental organization

PGRC/E   Plant Genetic Resources Centre Ethiopia
PTA   Projecto Tecnologia Alternativa (Brazil)
RAFI   Rural Advancement Foundation International
SADCC   Southern African Development Coordination
Conference
SEARICE   Southeast Asia Regional Institute for Community
Education (Philippines)
SEMOC   Sementes do Moçambique Limitada
TNC   Transnational corporation
TREE   Technology for Rural and Ecological Enrichment
(Thailand)
UNCED   UN Conference on Environment and Development
(Geneva, Rio de Janeiro 1992)
UNEP   UN Environment Programme (Nairobi)
UNESCO   UN Educational, Scientific and Cultural Organization
(Paris)
UPOV   Union for the Protection of New Varieties of Plants
(Geneva)
USC/C   Unitarian Service Committee Canada
WALHI   Wahana Lingkungan Hidup Indonesia (an NGO)
WIPO   World Intellectual Property Organisation (Geneva, UN)
ZSAN   Zimbabwe Seeds Action Network

A guide to technical, unfamiliar or strange-sounding terms used in this book

accession   An individual sample of seeds or plants entered into a germplasm collection in a genebank; used interchangeably with the term 'sample'. For example, one accession of maize in a genebank will be made of a number of seeds of one specific variety or population.

biodiversity   Biological diversity: all the varied forms of plants, animals and micro-organisms.

Brassica   The cabbage family, including kale, mustard and broccoli.

centre of diversity   In strict terms, refers to a geographical area identified by one of various scientists (for example, Vavilov, Zohary, Harlan) as a zone where there is a concentration of variation in genetic characteristics. Often used loosely by the authors here to designate any ecosystem particularly rich in genetic differentiation.

circa situ   Literally 'near site'. Used to refer to on-farm conservation where local genetic diversity is maintained not in the wild but within a production system.

cultivar A cultivated variety of plant; used interchangeably with the term 'variety'.

dicotyledonous A type of plant having two seed leaves.

DNA library A collection of genetic material as biochemical material, sometimes supposed to have potential to be a futuristic, high-tech conservation system where individual genes, rather than plants, may be stored.

élite Describing landraces or other forms of germplasm, to indicate an advanced level of stability and purity with respect to the desired result.

enhance Refers to the improvement of germplasm.

ex situ Literally 'off site'. Refers to genetic resources conservation outside of an ecosystem, most commonly a genebank.

extension The process whereby institutional scientific results are brought and transmitted to the farmer.

F2 The second filial generation in a breeding programme. The first cross between two parents gives rise to F1 offspring; when crossed, F1 offspring give rise to F2 progeny, and so on.

folkseed A term used to replace the word 'landrace' in order to recognize the fact that farmers or rural communities bred them.

formal system General term used in this book to refer to genebanks and professional researchers and breeders of governments and commercial companies.

genebank A cold-storage chamber or refrigerator where seeds are conserved under controlled conditions for future needs.

genepool The total number of genes available for crossing in breeding programmes.

genetic resources In a strict sense, the physical germplasm (hereditary material) which carries the genetic characteristics of life forms. In a broad sense, the germplasm plus information, funds, technologies and social and environmental systems through which germplasm is a socio-economic resource.

germplasm The material support of heredity.

hybrid Commonly speaking, any cross between two distinct things. In plant breeding it can be used two ways: to describe the offspring of any cross between two parents, be they varieties or species, or to designate specifically the first generation offspring (F1) of inbred varieties that normally produce an exceptionally high yield and cannot be re-used as seed the next season (because they lose this yield potential or are sterile). In this book, we have restricted the use of the term to the second case only.

informal system   General term used in this book to refer to farmers, their organizations and other NGOs in plant genetic resources conservation and improvement.

in situ   Literally 'on site'. Until recently, it was narrowly used to describe conservation of genetic resources in their natural surrounding, normally protected from human interference. However, it is increasingly used, as in this book, to designate conservation on the farm, where genetic resources are developed, bred and maintained.

intercropping   The planting of one crop into or among another, either between rows or into the remains of a previous crop.

introgression   The flow and exchange of genes between plant populations.

IR-(number)   Specific rice varieties developed by the International Rice Research Institute (IRRI).

landrace   A cultivated variety developed by farmers, usually a complex, heterogeneous genetic population.

mass selection   A simple breeding technique whereby the best individuals are picked out and retained for further breeding or seed production.

monocotyledonous   A type of plant having one seed leaf; includes all the cereals.

poor man's crop   The many crops which have local or regional importance and are usually ignored by formal scientific research of international trade.

population   In genetics, a group of individuals which share a common genepool and can interbreed. Traditional planting materials used by Third World farmers are usually referred to as populations because they are heterogeneous, as opposed to the pure lines produced by research centres or industry.

pure line   A highly uniform crop variety composed of nearly identical, homogeneous individuals.

rejuvenate   In *ex situ* conservation, to grow-out or regenerate a seed stock which is losing its capacity to germinate and may die.

sample   See *accession*.

seed bank   Terminology used in this book to distinguish a small, community-level genebank (seed store) from a large institutional one.

selection   Any process used to sift out certain genotypes rather than others; breeding.

Striga A weed that infests fields of small grains such as millet or sorghum in the semi-arid tropics.

tiller A shoot or stalk of a cereal plant.

tissue culture The multiplication of plant cells in a controlled environment. A simple form of biotechnology.

tungro A devastating rice-plant virus transmitted by hoppers.

variety A grouping of plants within a species which share common characteristics; used interchangeably with the term 'cultivar'.

Vavilov centre One of the eight centres of diversity identified by N.I. Vavilov.

Vigna A broad leguminous family including the cowpea and mung bean.

Addresses

Many of the contributors to this book are working with non-governmental organizations (NGOs) that are involved in issues relating to genetic resources and sustainable agriculture. Following is a brief description and their addresses. They might be able to help you with further information and other contacts to strengthen your own work.

Centro Internazionale Crocevia is an Italian project NGO which supports grassroots genetic resource projects in Burkina Faso, Mozambique, Nicaragua, Ecuador and the Philippines. Crocevia is also active in promoting public awareness campaigns on biodiversity.
Contact: Antonio Onorati or Andrea Gaifami, Crocevia, Via Ferraironi 88/G, I-00172 Rome, Italy. Tel: (39-6) 241 39 76; Fax: (39-6) 542 16 49.

CLADES (Consorcio Latinoamericano sobre Agroecologia y Desarrollo) is a coalition of NGOs promoting sustainable appoaches to rural development. CLADES and its member groups produce technical and training materials and work to raise awareness on related economic and political issues.
Contact: Camila Montecinos, CET, Casilla 97, Correo 9, Santiago, Chile. Tel: (56-2) 234 11 41; Faz: (56-2) 233 89 18; E-mail (GeoNet): GEO2:CLADES.

ENDA-Zimbabwe is part of the ENDA-TM (Environment and Development Action in the Third World) Network, based in Dakar, Senegal. ENDA-Zimbabwe conducts farmer-based genetic resources projects in conjunction with other local NGOs in Zimbabwe and the SADCC region.
Contact: Andrew Mushita, ENDA-Zimbabwe, PO Box 3492, Harare, Zimbabwe. Tel: (263-4) 70 85 68/9; Fax: (263-4) 70 51 21.

Genetic Resources Action International (GRAIN) promotes a worldwide campaign for the popular control of plant genetic resources. GRAIN is active in public information work and in lobbying for policy change on: enhancing community-based management of plant genetic resources; campaigning against patents and other forms of monopoly control over genetic resources; reforming the formal research and conservation sectors.
Contact: Henk Hobbelink, Renée Vellvé or David Cooper, GRAIN, Jonqueres 16, 6º D, 08003 Barcelona, Spain. Tel: (34-3) 310 59 09; Fax: (34-3) 310 59 52; E-mail (GeoNet): GEO2:GRAIN.

KENGO (Kenyan Energy and Environment Organizations) is a coalition of farmers' organizations, other NGOs and individuals working to promote sustainable natural resource use in Kenya.
Contact: Achoka Awori or Monica Opole, KENGO, PO Box 48197, Nairobi, Kenya. Tel: (254-2) 74 97 47; Fax: (254-2) 74 93 82.

Rural Advancement Foundation International (RAFI) is engaged in information work on policy issues in genetic diversity and lobbies relevant UN agencies. RAFI also has collaborative programmes to promote the conservation and use of traditional plant varieties in Africa, Asia and Latin America.
Contact: Pat Mooney, RAFI, 130 Slater Street, Suite 750, Ottawa, Ontario K1P 6E2, Canada. Tel: (1-613) 565 09 00; Fax: (1-613) 594 87 05; E-Mail (GeoNet): GEO4:RAFICAN.

RFSTNRP (Rural Foundation for Science, Technology and Natural Resource Policy) conducts policy research on farmer-based genetic resource work in India.
Contact: Vandana Shiva, 108 Ralpur Road, Dehra Dun 248001, India. Tel: (91-135) 23374; Fax: (91-135) 28392.

SEARICE (South-East Asia Regional Institute for Community Education) promotes community control over natural resources through training conferences, workshops and the projects of its member groups.
Contact: Rene Salazar, SEARICE, PO Box EA-31, Ermita, Manila, Philippines. Tel: (63-2) 96 90 71; Fax: (63-2) 521 13 19; E-mail (GeoNet): GEO2:ACCESS.

Swissaid campaigns in Switzerland on genetic diversity and intellectual property rights and supports farmer-based genetic resources projects, mostly in Latin America and Asia.
Contact: Miges Baumann, Swissaid, Jubiläumsstr. 60, CH-3000 Bern 6, Switzerland. Tel: (41-31) 44 95 55; Fax: (41-31) 43 27 83.

TREE (Technology for Rural and Ecological Enrichment) works to promote the use of traditional crop varieties in Thailand and to

challenge the harmful development policies of the government and multinational agricultural companies.
Contact: Day-cha Siripatra, TREE, 70/145 Soi 13, Prachanivate 2, Muang, Nonthaburi 11000, Thailand. Tel: (66-2) 573 12 64; Fax: (66-2) 226 47 18.

Selected reading

Periodicals
African Diversity, published by the African Committee for Plant Genetic Resources, reports on developments in the fields of biological diversity, biotechnology and plant genetic resources of signficance to Africa. Available from Seeds of Survival, PO Box 5977, Addis Ababa, Ethiopia.

Diversity is one of the most popular regular magazines covering genetic resources conservation worldwide and the related political, economic and social issues. A recent special issue, devoted solely to Latin America (Volume 7, Nos 1/2, 1991), and available in Spanish and English, contains articles looking at national programmes, regional co-operation and genetic erosion. Of particular interest is the contribution by Stephen B. Brush 'Farmer Conservation of New World Crops: the Case of Andean Potatoes' (pp. 82–6). Available from Diversity, 727 8th Street NW, Washington DC, 20003 USA.

ILEIA Newsletter, published quarterly by the Information Centre for Low External Input and Sustainable Agriculture, reports on grassroots initiatives and other projects in sustainable agriculture. Of particular interest is Volume 5, issue 4, December 1989: 'Local Varieties are Our Source of Health and Strength'. Available from ILEIA, Kastanjelaan 5, PO Box 64, 3830 AB Leusden, The Netherlands.

Seedling is the bulletin of Genetic Resources Action International, and carries feature articles on conservation initiatives in the Third World, seed industry updates, and reports and analysis of major trends in such things as genetic resources management, intellectual property rights, as well as regular news from the NGO network and book reviews. Available from GRAIN, Jonqueres 16, 6⁰ D, 08003 Barcelona, Spain.

There is a number of periodicals from Third World NGOs on general issues of sustainable agriculture. Amongst these are: *Minka*, a Peruvian magazine on peasant science and technology (in Spanish), available from Grupo Talpuy, Apartado 222, Huancayo, Peru; *Cuadernos Informativos* and *Hoja Informativa*, of the Committee for the Co-ordination of Andean Technology (in Spanish), available from CCTA, Apartado 14.0426, Lima 14, Peru; and *Resources*, covering environmental issues with a focus on Kenya, available from KENGO, PO Box 48197, Nairobi, Kenya.

Books and monographs

Biological Diversity and Innovation: Conserving and Utilizing Genetic Resources in Kenya (1989), by Calestous Juma, presents an overview of the role of genetic resources in Kenya's history and an analysis of the country's genetic resources conservation policy. It includes a survey of informal innovation by local farmers in the Bungoma district; legal and policy issues and biotechnology are discussed in the national context. Available from ACTS, PO Box 45917, Nairobi, Kenya.

Biotechnology and the Future of Agriculture (1991), by Henk Hobbelink of GRAIN, is a recent popular book on how the genetic technologies are being forged, by whom and in what directions, and their likely impact on farmers in the Third World. Available from Zed Books Ltd, 57 Caledonian Road, London N1 9BU, United Kingdom. (ISBN: 0-86232-837-3)

Community Seedbank Kit (1986), by the Rural Advancement Foundation International, is a theoretical and practical resource kit on community-based conservation of genetic resources, intended primarily for NGOs active in the Third World. (English, French, Portuguese and Spanish). Available from RAFI, PO Box 1029, Pittsboro, NC 27312, USA.

Farmer First: Farmer Innovation and Agricultural Research (1989), edited by Robert Chambers, Arnold Pacey and Lori Ann Thrupp, argues that agricultural research policies should start with farmers' own capacity for innovation and involve their active participation. It draws upon a range of case studies and experiences presented by social scientists, agriculturalists and economists from North and South to back up its case. Available from Intermediate Technology Publications, 103–105 Southampton Row, London WC1B 4HH, United Kingdom. (ISBN: 1-85339-007-0)

Joining Farmers' Experiments (1991), edited by Bertus Haverkort, Johan van der Kamp and Ann Waters-Bayer, looks at farmer innovation and grassroots technology development in developing countries. It is based on the proceedings of a workshop at the ILEIA centre in 1988 and brings together a range of experiences in research and technology development on low external-input sustainable agriculture based on farmers' experimental trials and evaluation. Available from Intermediate Technology Publications, 103–105 Southampton Row, London WC1B 4HH, United Kingdom. (ISBN 1-85339-101-8)

Recursos genéticos, nuestro tesoro olvidado: approximación técnica y socioeconómica (1988), by Daniel Querol, is a practical guidebook on conservation of plant genetic resources written by a Peruvian geneticist with much experience in setting up local conservation programmes in Third World countries. It begins with a global analysis of genetic diversity and international efforts to safeguard and improve genetic resources, followed by a thorough presentation of how to go about collecting and conserving plant genetic resources. (Spanish.) Available from GRAIN, Jonqueres 16, 6⁰ D, 08003 Barcelona, Spain.

The Threatened Gene – Food, Politics and the Loss of Genetic Diversity (1991), by Cary Fowler and Pat Mooney of RAFI, surveys the work of hunter-gatherers and farmers over the ages in the enhancement of genetic diversity, its erosion due to present-day policies and practices, the increasing corporate control of genetic resources in the age of biotechnology and the alternatives. Available from Lutterworth Press, PO Box 60, Cambridge CB1 2NT, United Kingdom. (ISBN: 0-7188-2830-5)

Staying Alive: Women, Ecology and Development (1989), by Vandana Shiva, examines the position of women in relation to natural resources, and links the violation of nature with the marginalization of women, especially in the Third World. The impact of science, technology and politics on women and biodiversity is examined. Available from Zed Books Ltd, 57 Caledonian Road, London N1 9BU, United Kingdom. (ISBN: 0-86232-823-3)

Technology Options and the Gene Struggle (1991), by Trygve Berg, Asmund Bjornstad, Cary Fowler and Tore Skroppa of NorAgric (the Norwegian Centre for International Agriculture Development), covers the science and politics of plant breeding, surveys the pros and cons of the formal and informal sectors and calls for an integrated approach to plant breeding. Available from NorAgric, The Library, PO Box 2, N-1432, Aas-NLH, Norway.

Technology Systems for Small Farmers: Issues and Options (1989), edited by Abbas M. Kesseba of the International Fund for Agricultural Development, addresses the question of how research can be better focused on the needs of the small farmer and whether traditional farming methods, skills and practices can be integrated with new technology systems. The contributors consider how productivity on smallholder farms can be improved through the use of better research systems and the development of economically viable and appropriate technologies. Available from Westview Press, 5500 Central Avenue, Boulder, CO 80301 USA. (ISBN 0-8133-7925-3)

Reports, briefings, technical publications and policy papers
'Status and Trends in Grassroots Crop Genetic Conservation Efforts in Latin America' (1991), by Camila Montecinos and Miguel Altieri, is a paper produced as a contribution to the WRI/ IUCN/UNEP Biodiversity Strategy Programme. It surveys the value of traditional plants in Latin America and farmers' efforts to conserve them. It provides a useful analysis of the technical problems faced by grassroots initiatives. Available from CLADES, Casilla 97, Correo 9, Santiago, Chile.

'Seeds and Genetic Resources in Kenya', by KENGO, gives an overview of Kenya's heritage of traditional trees and crop plants, current grassroots attempts to conserve them, and the impact of biotechnology and the privatization of seed companies. Available from KENGO, PO Box 48917, Nairobi, Kenya.

Proceedings of the Asian Regional Workshop on PGR Conservation and Development and the Impact of Related Technologies (1988), held in Indonesia in 1987, discusses grassroots strategies for genetic resources conservation in India, Sri Lanka, Thailand, Malaysia and the Philippines, and evaluates the impact of the new biotechnologies on farmers of the region. Available from SEA-RICE, PO Box EA-31, Ermita, Manila, Philippines.

Two issues of *Genes for Sustainable Development: Briefing on Biodiversity* have been produced by GRAIN. The first, published in October 1990, gives background information on biodiversity and the proposed global Convention for the Conservation and Utilization of Biological Diversity; the second, published in February 1991, discusses three key issues: access to genetic resources; technology transfer; and measures to improve the benefits at the community level. Available from GRAIN, Jonqueras 16, 6⁰ D, 08003 Barcelona, Spain.

An important document is the *Biodiversity Strategy and Action Plan*. It has been produced by a coalition of organizations led by IUCN, the World Resources Institute (WRI) and UNEP. It calls for a decade of action to save, study and use biodiversity. It contains a good section on improving the local benefits of biodiversity. Available from: Dr Kenton Miller, WRI, 1709 New York Avenue NW, Washington, DC 20006, USA.

Another important policy proposal is the *Global Initiative for the Security and Sustainable Use of Plant Genetic Resources*, the consensus report of the third and final plenary session of the Keystone International Dialogue on Plant Genetic Resources, Oslo, June 1991. It contains important conclusions and recommendations from the group drawn from diverse backgrounds: genebanks, industry, NGOs, governments and UN agencies. The contributors conclude that there are serious drawbacks with the present formal system of conservation and that greater recognition and support must be given to the informal sector. They caution against the extension of the patent system in GATT and put forward detailed proposals for an institutional framework and funding for a global initiative. Available from the Keystone Center, PO Box 606, Keystone, CO 84035 USA. A book based on the Keystone Process is being prepared under the auspices of the Dag Hammarskjöld Foundation and should be available during 1992. Contact the Dag Hammarskjöld Foundation, Ovre Slottsgatan 2, S-75220 Uppsala, Sweden.

At a more technical level, the *Gatekeeper Series*, an occasional publication of the Sustainable Agriculture Programme of the IIED, covers issues such as indigenous knowledge systems and participatory approaches to agricultural development. Of particular interest are No. 19 'Crop Variety Mixtures in Marginal Environments' by Janice Higgins, and No. 22 'Microenvironments Unobserved' by Robert Chambers. A full list of issues available can be obtained from IIED, 3 Endsleigh Street, London WC1H 0DD, United Kingdom.

The *Agricultural Administration (Research and Development) Network* of the Overseas Development Institute, London, produces a series of network and discussion papers on issues such as participatory approaches and seed diffusion systems. No. 22 in this series: 'Farmer Participation in On-farm Varietal Trials' (December 1987), by Jacqueline Ashby, describes the approach of one research team at CIAT, Colombia, to involve farmers in the evaluation and selection of plant breeding programmes. A list is available from ODI-AAN, Regent's College, Regent's Park, London NW1 4NS, United Kingdom.

Video

A 30-minute VHS-PAL Video, *Participatory Research with Women Farmers* (1991), by Michel Pimbert, describes how the involvement of farmers in plant breeding programmes leads to more effective research in meeting farmers' needs. Available from ICRISAT Information Services, Patancheru PO, Andhra Pradesh 502 324, India.

Notes

Chapter 5

1. Murdock, G.P. and White, D.C., 'Standard Cross-cultural Sample', *Ethnology*, Vol. 8, 1969, pp. 329–69.
2. Usha, M.S., *Women: The Forgotten Sector in Hill Development*, paper presented to the seminar on 'Women and Development' organized by the National Institute of Public Cooperation and Child Development, Regional Centre of Lucknow, 9–11 February 1984.
3. Bhata and Singh, 'Women's Contribution to Agricultural Economy in Hill Regions of Northwest India', *Economic and Political Weekly*, Delhi, Vol. 22.

Chapter 8

1. Vavilov, N.I., 'The Origin, Variation, Immunity and Breeding of Cultivated Plants', *Chronica Botanical*, Vol. 13, pp. 1–366.
2. Frankel, O.H., 'Genetic Resources Surveys as a Basis for Exploration', *Crop Genetic Resources for Today and Tomorrow*, O.H. Frankel and J.G. Hawkes (eds), IBP2, Cambridge University Press, 1973, pp. 99–109; Zohary, D., 'Centres of Diversity and Centres of Origin', in *Genetic Resources in Plants, Their Exploration and Conservation*, O.H. Frankel and E. Bennet (eds), Blackwell Scientific, Oxford, 1970, pp. 33–42.

Chapter 10

1. Francis, C.A., *Multiple Cropping Systems*, MacMillan, New York, 1986.
2. Clawson, D.L., 'Harvest Security and Intra-specific Diversity in Traditional Tropical Agriculture', *Economic Botany*, 1985, Vol. 39, 56–67.
3. Wilkes, H.G., 'Mexico and Central America as a Centre for the Origin of Agriculture and the Evolution of Maize', *Economic Botany*, 1979, Vol. 31, pp. 254–293.
4. Altieri, M.A. *et al.*, 'The Ecological Role of Weeds in Insect Pest Management Systems: A Review Illustrated with Bean Cropping Systems', *Pest Articles News and Summaries* (PANS), 1977, Vol. 23, pp. 195–205.
5. Contreras, A.M., 'Germoplasma chileno de papas', *Anales Simposia Recursos Fitogenéticos*, UACH-IBPGR, Valdivia, 1987.